STRUT

STRUT

How Every Woman Can Be a Leader of Change

SAMAR SHERA

Published by Grand Harbor Press, Grand Haven, MI

www.brilliancepublishing.com

ISBN-13: 9781542046343
ISBN-10: 1542046343

Cover design by Faceout Studio

Printed in the United States of America

To all women and children who have ever been bullied, burned, silenced, violated, abused, or displaced.

May my life's work help eradicate every form of disempowerment from human consciousness.

When sleeping women wake, mountains move.

—Chinese proverb

CONTENTS

Author's Note

In the client narratives discussed herein, all clients' names, the names and sometimes the gender of other participants in the narrative, and all incidental information have been changed for confidentiality. In some instances, the content of several cases has been combined into a single story for instructional purposes.

Introduction

Women are in the midst of transformational times. We are *all* in this together, whether we choose to believe it or not. And to change the path that we—both as individuals and as part of the global community—are on, we will have to step into our true selves as Leaders of Change.

As women, you and I may have much in common. But it's likely that we come from different backgrounds. I was born and grew up in Dubai, a thriving urban center in the United Arab Emirates, as the daughter of Pakistani Muslim immigrants who arrived with a meager seven thousand rupees in their pockets. Hoping to provide better educational opportunities for my brothers and me, my parents worked tirelessly to transform the little they had into a flourishing business. I attended private, internationally minded schools, studying among students from families that practiced a variety of religions. Together we thrived.

I proudly call Dubai my home and would not be where I am today without the courage and ambition of immigrant parents, as well as the Dubai state of mind, which nurtures greatness and growth and encourages its citizens to also be citizens of the world, while maintaining their values, integrity, and sense of self. Here people of different religions and from different backgrounds peacefully coexist—a fact marred by the media much too often.

Contrary to a commonly held stereotype about Muslim countries, both boys and girls are provided an excellent education in the United Arab Emirates. In fact, the literacy rate for both men and women in Dubai is close to 95 percent.[1] The UAE aims to be one of the top twenty-five countries for gender equality by 2021.[2] Here, women are educated, given equal job opportunities, and can have financial independence if they so choose.

In 2000, I left for university in the UK to study accounting and finance. I was happy in my studies, and I'd hoped to return to Dubai and use what I was learning to contribute to my parents' business. But everything changed on September 11, 2001. When those planes crashed into the World Trade Center, I watched with horror along with the rest of the world. I was forced to ask myself a question I hadn't thought of before: How could any religion or ideology be used to justify the atrocious killings of innocent people?

All of a sudden I felt intensely driven to *understand* religion, to explore how some people use it to justify violence and oppression. Soon after my first degree was complete, I enrolled in a world-renowned theology school in London in hopes of an answer.

I stripped myself of everything I'd been taught so that I could learn with a clear mind and an open heart. I read the writings of philosophers such as Nietzsche, Freud, and Jung and delved into

---

1 "Education in the UAE," Embassy of the United Arab Emirates, accessed April 11, 2017, http://www.uae-embassy.org/about-uae/education-uae.

2 "UAE Aims to Reach Top 25 in Gender Equality by 2021," Khaleej Times, May 2, 2016, http://www.khaleejtimes.com/nation/government/uae-aims-to-reach-top-25-in-gender-equality-by-2021.

the multitude of musings surrounding God and religion. Before long I started to see the commonalities shared by the major religions of the world, even religions at war with each other. These commonalities far outweigh the differences, which people tend to focus on. Over time, religion has become a personal, bodily experience for me, rather than a repetition of someone else's words—an inward journey that transformed me. A journey that continues till this very day and that perhaps doesn't end.

After earning a degree in theology and religious studies with a focus on philosophy of religion, I returned to Dubai. But my journey into the human mind, heart, and soul was not over. Along with conventional methods, I began to study alternative modalities and therapies, including integrated clinical hypnotherapy, past-life regression, karma, family dynamics, and the connection between physical disease and thought patterns. I delved into meditation and stillness practices and the teachings of Osho, Jiddu Krishnamurti, *A Course in Miracles*, and existential psychotherapy. The works of Irvin Yalom still reside on my bedside table.

When I began to build my own family, I ventured into productivity and time-management studies. I had professional and personal ambitions, and I wanted to take care of my family too. This took me to the US, where I trained with leaders in the field of personal development. As I had in London, I again saw how similar we all are, regardless of our backgrounds, belief systems, or geographical locations.

In April 2015, my cousin Sabeen Mahmud was assassinated. She was a human-rights activist in Pakistan and the founder of the Second Floor (now called T2F), an organization dedicated to open and peaceful dialogue. She was shot point-blank driving home from a community forum about the missing people of Balochistan.

While so many world leaders preach hatred and bigotry from the world stage, hers was a voice for collaboration, for resolution that would serve everyone. For that notion she was silenced.

Losing Sabeen increased my determination to shine a light on the hand that we as women have been dealt—and to remind women that we are powerful, that we must speak up, that our voices must be heard. The most valuable gift I have to offer is the wisdom I've gained through my journey. In no way do I claim to represent any group to which I belong or anyone other than myself. I disclose only my own personal experience—all other stories are altered so that no individual can be identified from them. I use the insight I've gained, alongside the modalities I've studied, to work with women of every race, religion, nationality, and creed to help them gain a deeper sense of themselves.

You can expect the truth from me and that I'll push you a little (or a lot) to gain insight into yourself at a deeper level than you've dared venture before. I want you to catch a glimpse of your true self and feel safe enough to manifest her in all her glory. The world needs our truth—yours and mine—to be discovered and expressed. This is vital to the survival of all of us and the world as we know it.

This book has evolved over the years as I've undergone my own personal-development work and work with other women. *You* and women like you are my primary source of inspiration. Though our stories differ, our journey is the same—back to our own selves, to our truest form of being.

If you're not interested in real, deep change, I recommend you put down this book. Because if you put this paradigm-shifting information into action, you will be changed. I am not talking about magical thinking or pep talks with no practical application or result. Our thoughts are indeed powerful, but mere thinking is insufficient. Meditating solely on what we want, without being fully connected to the greater good, leaves us ungrounded and is self-serving. Instead I invite you to open your mind and heart to a more profound path that will empower you not only to take ownership of your own life but to bring change to others and to a world that desperately needs healing and direction.

Recently my seven-year-old son asked me, "Mom, what is more important: freedom or safety?" I would like to think it's freedom. Freedom in a world where women—and all people—are safe, a world where women won't have to risk their lives to speak up.

That world doesn't exist yet, but it could. Those of us lucky enough to be relatively safe, to have a roof over our heads and warm food in our bellies, must step up. We have a duty to those who are despairing and displaced, fleeing in rubber boats or selling their bodies or their children to stave off starvation. We progress as a gender either in entirety or not at all.

It starts inside. The journey inward ultimately brings us back to our community and helps us create lives that make us proud and take actions that ripple outward to impact global society.

May this book be of service to those who have just begun to ask the question "How can I change myself so that I can change the world?" and to those who are already engaged in personal transformation and want to take it a step further. You have the potential to be a Leader of Change, if you dare to create the life and the world you want. I offer this book in service to you on your journey.

Chapter One

We Are Born to Strut

From Tragedy to Transformation

One morning I walked into my preschool classroom and, pausing in the doorway, waited for everyone to look at my diva-esque pose.

And they did.

After all, I was wearing my mom's yellow kitten heels. Hands on my hips, I strutted to my seat in those oversized shoes that clicked crisply against the cold floor with every step. My gray skirt swayed as I whisked my hair over my shoulder. I was rockin' it. Jaws dropped and excitement spread as the children pointed at my heels. Oohs and aahs filled the air.

I may have been only three years old, but I had everyone's attention, not simply with the shoes on my feet but with my confidence. I was in charge of myself, and even though I was small in size, I was large in power. During the walk from the door to my chair, for an oh-so-brief moment, I experienced life as it's meant to be. I was the leader of my own life, without hesitation. I instinctively knew how to strut.

Unfortunately, life has knocked me off my feet since then. Hard. Like most people, I have seen tragedy, disappointment, and betrayal. Add to that the many disempowering messages I received daily, and the strut was, day by day, taken out of my step.

We've all been knocked off our feet. There are moments when our lives stop—abruptly—and everything seems to go in slow motion. You've likely had those experiences—the life-altering moments when you got hurt as a little girl, your heart was first broken, you were let go from your job, you found out your husband was having an affair, or the medical report came back with the word "cancer." Everything changed in an instant, and you knew somewhere deep inside that your life would never be the same.

This moment came for me when I was in my late twenties. Until then, I'd been able to convince myself and the world that I was a woman at the top of her game. I excelled in school, married my high school sweetheart, and dove into a career that gave me material wealth and a sense of accomplishment. I excelled in my family's businesses—an advertising agency, several photography stores in the biggest shopping malls, and several souvenir stores in the grandest of hotels. I expanded our holdings by establishing a boutique supermarket with high-end international products. Life could not have been better. I was living the future my parents had planned for me. I strode in stilettos, head held high, portraying a self-assured woman, a woman at ease with herself. I fooled everyone—even myself.

Then one day, the other shoe dropped. I was stunned when my obstetrician said to me, "Here's a refund on your pregnancy package, Mrs. Shera."

"What do you mean, refund? I didn't ask for a refund. I'm still pregnant."

"I know. But we don't accept high-risk pregnancy cases. And you're high risk," the doctor responded oh so matter-of-factly.

"You put me through an amniocentesis. You've run dozens of tests. All the results came out clear. Doctor, I don't understand."

"Yes, they have come out clear. But there's still something wrong with your baby. We just don't know what."

Tears in my eyes, I mentally accused someone up there of playing a sick joke. "What am I supposed to do now?" I asked.

"Find a specialist."

I went straight home and called every hospital in Dubai. Our health-care system is highly ranked at twenty-seventh in the world,[3] yet I was told to seek specialist help abroad. I was referred to one of the world's leading experts in London.

My husband returned from work and found me in the living room. Before I could say a word, he announced, "Our landlord decided not to renew our lease."

My feet were killing me, and my heart was breaking. "When do we have to be out?"

"Tomorrow."

Within twenty-four hours, we found a new place to live, packed up our belongings, moved the boxes into our new apartment, and boarded a plane to the UK.

We landed in London at eight in the morning. The December cold penetrated my bones. In the specialist's office, we sat in a reception area, surrounded by pregnant women, with a few husbands

3 "World Health Organization Assesses the World's Health Systems," World Health Organization, last modified June 21, 2000, http://who.int/whr/2000/media_centre/press_release/en.

scattered into the mix. I hugged my arms tight around my belly to protect my baby girl, Lia. She was my first daughter, and Lia was the name I had always dreamed of giving her. Everyone in the waiting room was chitchatting in an attempt to keep spirits high, but nothing could mask the truth. We all knew that few, if any, of us were going to make it out of there without some bad news.

My husband and I waited for what seemed an eternity. Our appointment time of two o'clock came and went. Still we waited. One patient after another was called, but progress was slow. As the sun went down, my husband went out to find us some food. Rather than close the office at the end of the workday and tell those of us still waiting to return the following morning, the doctor and nurses stayed on. It wasn't until two in the morning, a full twelve hours after my scheduled appointment, that my name was finally called. My husband and I walked to the exam room at the end of the corridor.

Nervousness and fatigue were in the air. Two young nurses hovered around medical equipment, adjusting and readjusting to perfection. No doctor in sight. I was guided to every woman's favorite chair, where I sat down and put my feet up in the stirrups. The leather was cold against my skin. My body felt heavy as I mustered up the last iota of strength I had within me to endure another examination.

I turned my head to the right so I could see the screen. There was my baby. My beautiful daughter, who, I knew in my heart of hearts, would not live. The nurses chattered to themselves. A bubble of fluid enveloped the top half of the baby's body like nothing they had ever seen.

We all jumped a little when the doctor burst into the room. He walked quickly to the screen and started to shout out questions, boot-camp style, at the anxious nurses. I assumed his military demeanor was a defense mechanism that allowed him to stay sane while doling out bad news to mothers-to-be. Still, my usual sympathetic fight-for-the-underdog tendencies were starting to crumble under my exhaustion. The nurses were unable to answer his questions. He balked at their stupidity.

"Can't you see?" he yelled. We stared blankly at the screen. "The baby's not moving," he said. Like a ton of bricks, it was suddenly so obvious, staring us right in the face. "Have you seen the child move in any of your ultrasounds, Mrs. Shera?"

"No," I whispered as tears began to stream down my face.

"I'm sorry, Mrs. Shera. You carry a rare gene called fetal akinesia, which causes paralysis in the fetus. The buildup of water around the child is a side effect of the paralysis." He told me in less than two minutes what had left other doctors baffled. I was numb.

He continued, "Her arms are paralyzed across her chest, restricting her lung growth. She's suffocating slowly, Mrs. Shera. She's not going to make it to term. We can't risk you going into spontaneous labor. We have to put you through a D&C first thing in the morning."

I could barely breathe as each new revelation struck one blow after another to my very soul. I wasn't sure how much more I could endure. I mustered up the energy to ask one final question. I just had to. The not knowing would kill me.

"Will I be able to have children in the future?" I whispered.

"Mrs. Shera, your condition is genetic. You will struggle to have children all your life."

His words shattered my world.

Living in a Masculine World

Though beautiful in an infinite number of ways, the world is mired in violence, deceit, materialism, bigotry, and fear. Throw in gender inequality (sexual harassment, glass ceilings, the profitable perpetuation of low self-worth and self-esteem, and so forth), and the result is that our truest essence and the root of our power—our feminine potential—remains buried under a mound of shame, silence, abuse, unrealistic expectations, and fear.

This is a world operating within an overly masculine paradigm, in which societal hierarchy is standard, brute force reigns, and feelings are often viewed as little more than a nuisance. While masculine energy is not intrinsically dangerous, when it isn't balanced with feminine energy it can become quite destructive. Where you or I may land in the hierarchy determines the power we have over ourselves and those beneath us. The strong are on the top, and the weak or less influential are on the bottom. Within this paradigm there is not enough for everyone—not enough power, not enough access, not enough resources to go around. Decisions are made solely at the top, and the rest of us obey.

This model is dominant in most families, communities, organizations, businesses, and governments across the globe. In many cultures, women receive gender training from the moment they take their first breath. Most of us are taught to submit to our leaders, our fathers, and later our husbands. At its extreme, we see groups who refuse to allow girls to attend school for fear that they might develop aspirations beyond the roles of wife and mother. Within this suffocating system, many of us surrender our ability to chart our own course, instead going about our lives without questioning the paradigm within which we live.

Swinging to the other side of the pendulum is not the answer. It is common for those who want to empower women to do so by cultivating a mistrust or rejection of the masculine. But leading solely out of the feminine can be just as dangerous as leading solely out of the masculine. Basing choices exclusively on intuition and emotion can leave us ungrounded, lost in a private reality that others cannot share. We become obsessed with ourselves as individuals, incapable of making fair decisions or taking action on behalf of the collective. When the unbalanced feminine leads, our self-focused needs occupy excessive space in our own minds. Power comes into play, and the feminine takes on the form of the black widow who mates with and then devours her male counterpart. The feminine, when betrayed, can emerge as Hera, the mythical wife of Zeus, who rages at her husband's betrayals and seeks to destroy other women.

We must reject any paradigm that is out of balance, including one that restricts men to masculinity or women to femininity. Within this paradigm, we are each trained from day one to live in a predefined, gendered box. Ladies, take a look around. Even a cursory glance at magazine covers, bestselling books, highly rated TV shows, and social media feeds reveals a barrage of tips and expectations about our feminine wiles, about how we should use our intelligence and sexuality to get what we want—which apparently is to "have it all." Every day we are given the message that we should aspire to be nothing more than Barbie dolls who use our sexual charms to bag bread-winning men, that power is a measure of how seductive we can be while twirling our hair, speaking in high pitches, and sprinkling our sentences with the word "like" one too many times.

Even if, despite the odds, you work your way up the corporate ladder, it's likely that you've done so at the expense of your authenticity by adhering to the rules of a masculine world. To make it in a man's world, we have to play by masculine rules. Yet there is no escape, since we as a culture will judge women either way: if you act "feminine," people don't listen to you or they doubt your competency, and if you act "masculine"—meaning in a way similar to male peers—people say you're "angry" or "ball busting" or "unapproachable." And it seems that no matter what we do, folks will call us "shrill" and grade our bodies on a scale of one to ten. Damned if you do, damned if you don't.

No matter where we land on the social ladder, for most of us a primary benchmark of achievement is money. How much is there in the bank account? How much will this project make me? How many zeros can I acquire on my paycheck? When we allow money to define our success, we ultimately end up sacrificing ourselves for an ever-elusive goal. This keeps us in the cycle of validating our self-esteem through external things—money, cars, bank accounts—at the expense of the greater good, the planet. Not to mention the basics, like health, positive relationships, and happiness. It serves many in power to have us on this hamster wheel, distracting us from our own potential.

Now the planet and the new paradigm of thought coming forth are asking for something new. Because let's be honest: No amount of money is ever enough. We can never be beautiful enough or sexy enough or smart enough. And if we pass the self-loathing torch to future generations, if we teach them from a young age to join the facade, to endure pain with smiles on their faces, to pursue goals that won't make them happy, all the while sacrificing what they feel truly called to do, we are only maintaining this prison for our jailers. And why would we want to do that?

So what can we do to make the world a better place? Sometimes it feels as though the answer is "Nothing." But is that true? Don't we all want to contribute to the betterment of the world we live in, for ourselves, our families, the rest of the planet, and future generations? We as women may not be in an equitable number of positions of traditional power, yet I refuse to believe that we are in a position of powerlessness. We have been deemed ordinary when we are truly the extraordinary, the visionary, the intuitive, the game changers. I encourage you to reject the notion that we are not up to the task of personal and global transformation. So what *can* we do?

We can wake up.

Tragedy to Transformation

My tragedy sent me on a quest that transformed my life. After the loss of my baby, I searched for a way to cope with the intense depression and heartache that, at that point, defined my life. I did not recover from the loss by working through layers of grief, but my entire life and how I live it was redefined. I had to change everything: how I understood the world and my place in it as a woman; how I experienced life; and how I saw and related to myself. For the first time I began to scratch the surface of my own disempowerment—and to recognize that I was not alone in the systemic disempowerment suffered by women worldwide.

We never really get over a tragedy. I can never get my baby back. The truth is, we can never return to the way life was or be the women we were before we were knocked off our feet. Every attempt to go back to the past is futile.

Though we may know this on some level, many women do not fully accept this reality, and instead they fruitlessly dedicate themselves to the goal of re-creating the past. As a result, they waste their lives, using all their energy trying to do the impossible. We are intended to be transformed by these tragedies so that we can live our lives on an entirely different plane—one of power and confidence. Resisting transformation is like a psychic dragging of your heels. Certainly it is an option. But is it the best one in terms of your survival? If you refuse to learn, you place yourself in a position of powerlessness, of fear. And fear makes it impossible to lead.

Despair, even hopelessness, can signal being on the cusp of change. If we rise to the occasion and meet ourselves on the path of transformation, we stand as viable creators of something long lasting, real, and sustainable. You're never too old for self-transformation—I embarked on this journey in my late twenties, and I can only imagine the ripple effect of more and more women choosing this journey, to the point that girls are born into a world that is conducive to their success, personal growth, well-being, and emotional health. It is up to us to bring this change about.

Rania's Story

Rania came to me one day, her eyes swollen from a long night of crying. She'd just discovered her husband's affair, and she was shattered to her very core. Her family was the center of her world, and she felt like everything she'd built had come crumbling down as soon as she'd laid eyes on those text messages. Questions flitted through her mind at the speed of light, so fast that she couldn't keep up. *Does he want a divorce? What will happen to the kids? Who will get custody? How will the children handle it? What will I do to support myself? Will I be alone for the rest of my life? Did the last ten years mean nothing to him?*

Rania seriously considered staying silent about the affair. The risk was high—if she spoke up, she might be left penniless and alone, separated from her children. And so Rania's effort to sift through her emotions took a great deal of courage. In doing so, she realized that it was not about what her husband wanted but about what *she* wanted—a question she had not asked herself in years.

Rania loved her family dearly, but over time she'd lost herself in the responsibilities of being a wife and mother. Before marriage and motherhood, she'd had an intense passion for interior design and a general love of life. Now she found herself in a position of subservience, with her husband holding the reins of their relationship. She'd forgotten to nurture other aspects of who she was.

Rania decided it was time to take her power back, to rekindle her passion. This brave woman used her tragedy as a vehicle for transformation and never looked back. Soon after, her husband confessed that during his affair he'd been looking for the confident go-getter that Rania had been, the woman he had fallen for in the first place—and that he'd made a terrible mistake.

There was a lot of healing to be done, and together they worked hard to rebuild their marriage. Aside from her newfound confidence, Rania discovered a new level of intimacy with her husband, a better relationship with her kids (who couldn't have been happier to see her happy), and time to do the things she enjoyed.

Now imagine that Rania had chosen the path of silence. Not only would she have lived as a lesser version of herself, but she would have also taught her daughters to do the same. The ripple effect of our choices is vastly disregarded—rarely is the impact of our choices on others ever brought to attention. From the darkest depths of your personal hell, you can emerge armed with a flame that will light your path of transformation. This transformation begins internally and then moves outward into the external. More often than not, the internal shift is enough for you to create a change on the outside without any conscious intention of doing so.

You must work on the internal first. There is no point protesting a form of disempowerment in the world only to come home and continue your life with disempowered thoughts or within a disempowered relationship. The only way to move forward is to first alter your thought process. Yes, change starts within. And the key to that change is self-awareness.

Self-awareness is the root of empowerment. It is the ability to see what you've learned passively and what you've been taught—often referred to as "conditioning"—for what it is at any given moment, to understand when conditioning drives your reactions. Whether they come from teachers or parents, priests or rabbis, actors or models, programmed reactions keep us stuck in a vicious cycle in which we perpetually respond in the same old way, so no learning or growth can take place. This repetitive action, and its requisite pretense and resultant pain, continue like the same sad song track looping over and over and over.

Change requires unrelenting honesty about our true selves. Self-awareness is the process whereby you realize that you are using someone else's map and then decide to chart your own course instead, to take back the helm of your ship and figure out how to navigate the roughest seas of life. You are no longer reacting to situations based on subconscious patterns; instead, you are responding from a self-aware state. This allows you to create the life you want—and it starts with you and ends with you.

Self-awareness is never an individual act contained within itself. It ripples out far and wide, encouraging those around you to behave authentically. This is you acting as a Leader of Change, and the effect is much like an earthquake, with you as the epicenter. The aftershocks can crop up anywhere and everywhere—often catching you completely by surprise.

Leaders of Change

A Leader of Change is a woman who embodies her feminine potential, her true essence. She lives in and acts out of self-awareness, at peace with who she is and what she brings to the table. Aware that she has the power to lead her own life, she takes ownership of her choices, perceptions, and actions. Though it may seem easier to buckle under the pressures of a society that dictates who she should be and how she should behave, she refuses to live behind a facade, to disconnect from the authentic self in violation of her feminine essence.

It's up to you to make the most significant change you can make—in yourself. Being a Leader of Change will look different for everyone. The world is full of advice about looking inward, yet there is no road map. Everyone's journey is unique, one which we all must undertake alone. I don't offer you another script to say or mask to wear. What I can give you is a compass so that you know in which direction to look. By asking key self-reflective questions and being grounded in self-awareness, you will discover true empowerment, becoming who you are meant to be—your authentic self.

Here is where STRUT comes in. The method is simple:

S: Shift Your Mind-Set
T: Take Ownership of Your Life
R: Reconnect with Your Body
U: Unblock Your Feminine Potential
T: Take the Lead

The magnificence of STRUT is how it facilitates acting out of self-awareness and becoming your own version of a Leader of Change. You are released to express your individuality in whatever form it takes for you.

We must not miss the opportunity to be Leaders of Change. By setting our feminine potential free into the world, in balance with the masculine, we will give birth to an era in which human lives matter more than dollar bills, the starving children of the world are no longer a numbers game, the violation or displacement of women and children is not permissible on any level, and individual empowerment pulses through the veins of this new world.

A Word of Warning

In the next chapters, you will take a significant step toward resurrecting your authentic power. You will reconnect to the person you once were and who you are meant to be. This journey is not for the faint of heart. You'll be tempted to fall back into old patterns when it gets a little too personal or challenging.

Expect your internal resistance to show up. There will be days when you will scream, "I don't want to do this!" There will be other days when your mind will create so many diversions, you won't even pick up this book. There will be times when you will make other things more important than the change you so desire.

I want you to know this is perfectly normal. You see, your body is hardwired to maintain internal stability, also known as homeostasis, and your mind is hard at work categorizing and keeping you in the "known," the realm of the familiar, in which you've successfully survived before. So every time you step out of your comfort zone, an alarm bell will go off, and voices in your head will begin offering you a million and one reasons to stay within your secure place. You will tell yourself that you can't do it and that you shouldn't do it!

"What will other people think?" your resistance will whisper.

"What will your pastor, priest, imam, or other religious leader say?"

"You're going to disappoint people."

"You'll upset your husband."

"Your mother will not approve."

"You could lose your job!"

"You are just being selfish."

Plus a thousand more reasons. Sometimes you will outright believe you don't deserve to change and are not capable of it. Trust me, I know. I've been there. And as I gain a deeper sense of my feminine potential each day, I struggle too. But the rewards have proven to me that it's worth it.

Believe in yourself, and know that you have the right, even the responsibility, to make this choice. Become aware of these disempowering thoughts as they crop up throughout your day. Decide how much power you want to give them. Make a decision about this before you continue. It is my opinion that it is our birthright to have everything our hearts desire.

It may motivate you to move forward to realize that all the things you think you're so cleverly hiding from the rest of the world are actually plastered in neon lights across your forehead. Really. If you continue in self-defeating ways, you'll only be fooling yourself. No one is buying your act in the first place.

The first step to becoming a Leader of Change is to be self-aware of which mind-set you operate from, allowing you the power to shift it.

REFLECTION EXERCISES

The reflection exercises below, and those throughout the book, are intended to help you become more self-aware. Not all of them will be relevant to your situation, so use the ones that are helpful, and feel free to modify them in any way that speaks more directly to you and the way you process information. I encourage you to write down your thoughts.

- In the past, how has a tragedy or challenge caused you to rethink your world view?
- What tragedies or challenges are you facing right now?
- Which of these tragedies or challenges is causing you the most pain? Describe how you feel.
- How might this situation be pushing you in a new direction?
- In what area of your life are you hoping to grow?

Chapter Two

S = Shift Your Mind-Set

Two False Dichotomies: The Damsel and the Superwoman

After the D&C, I returned to an apartment that didn't feel like home, without the baby I had been carrying. I took to bed. Every morning, the ultimate struggle was to lift my head off the pillow. It was anyone's guess as to which would win: the emotional and spiritual pain bearing down on me like a crushing weight, or the obligation I felt to act as if nothing were wrong.

Dear God. It's me, Samar. Samar Shera. And you've handed me the wrong life.

The mornings I did manage to lift myself out of bed, I did what was expected of me: I put on a face for the world and acted as if everything were fine. "Don't worry. Your next baby will be healthy," said one of my family members. I felt like knocking him out but didn't. That would have blown my cover. I had no intention of letting my family see my pain, my sorrow, my rage. After all, I was the strong one.

So private was I at the time that I hadn't even told my friends that I'd been pregnant. Now, so determined to present myself as the invincible overachiever, I didn't have the nerve to tell them I had lost the baby. I hit rock bottom, dug a hole there, and settled in.

One particular morning—not that I actually cared that a new day had come—I lay motionless in bed. My arm hung off the side, and my body felt lifeless. Sunlight streamed in through the small window in the corner of the room. The funnel of light illuminated the dust lingering in the air.

God, this is your fault. There is no damn way this would have happened if you had not dealt me this horrible hand.

As I work with women from around the globe, among them those who identify as Christian, Hindu, agnostic, Buddhist, Muslim, atheist, secular humanist, mystical, and New Age spiritual, I find that many of us try to blame something or someone for our difficulties. I was no different at the time. I even had science on my side of the argument.

My genetic counselor informed me there was a one-in-five-million chance that a person could carry the fetal akinesia gene. The chances of two people carrying that one rare gene getting together were nearly impossible. At the time, there had been less than one hundred cases reported in the entire world.[4] A percentage of those

4 "Fetal Akinesia Deformation Sequence," Orphanet, last modified July 2005, http://www.orpha.net/consor/cgi-bin/OC_Exp.php?Lng=EN&Expert=994.

existed in relatives who had intermarried.[5] My husband and I were of different races, originating from different countries. How could such a thing happen to us? To me?

I was angry at life for playing this sick, twisted joke. Moreover, I was angry with myself for allowing my daughter to die. Surely I could have done something. And most certainly God or fate or even sheer luck could have tipped me off before it was too late. I wallowed in self-pity and seethed in anger for a few months behind closed doors. I desperately wanted someone to rescue me from my pain or erase the past and give me a do-over. But when I was in public (I had to emerge to make sure no one suspected anything was wrong), I was the picture of strength, seemingly unburdened and glowing with confidence.

After months of this turmoil, I started to watch myself. I saw myself swing from an intense sense of self-loathing and powerlessness on one side to a facade of superior womanhood on the other. In a matter of minutes, I'd declare to myself, "I can't take another day of this pain," only to contradict myself with "No one can defeat me! I'm Samar Shera!" With a flash of insight, I saw it clearly. And I wasn't at all happy with what I saw.

Two False Dichotomies

Most of us are locked in the grip of a self-destructive mind-set that forces us to choose between two false dichotomies. The human

---

5 Astrid Hellmund, Christoph Berg, Annegret Geipel, Annette Müller, and Ulrich Gembruch, "Prenatal Diagnosis of Fetal Akinesia Deformation Sequence (FADS): A Study of 79 Consecutive Cases," Archives of Gynecology and Obstetrics 294, no. 4 (October 2016): 697–707. doi: 10.1007/s00404-016-4017-x.

race at this time in history is woefully out of balance, immersed in a masculine-dominated global perspective while the feminine point of view is disempowered and suppressed. And so we as women are given two choices: become a Damsel or a Superwoman.

The Damsel

We are all acquainted with the Damsel. She is sweet, helpless, and in peril, calling for a man to save her. She has been infused into the collective psyche through stories passed down from generation to generation. Her presence colors the greatest tragedies, from fairy tales to Hollywood movies. Cinderella's story revolves around a prince fulfilling her dreams, and Snow White and Sleeping Beauty are both saved by the kiss of their one true love.

The Damsel is the quintessential victim. There is nothing more delightful to the imbalanced masculine than for a woman to be utterly dependent and vulnerable, as this provides the chance to play the knight in shining armor. I'm not saying that men, per se, consciously desire this kind of woman. There are many emotionally and spiritually mature men who reject the disparity so prevalent today. Yet we women are often pushed, coerced, or bullied by unquestioned thought patterns, religious attitudes, and societal paradigms into a place where we need to be "rescued."

Let me illustrate how the Damsel mind-set translates from her psyche into reality. In Damsel mode, she is stuck, responding to life from a place of helplessness or passivity. This is a disempowered place, where things happen *to* her. She suffers but does not act. She whines. She blames. She looks up at the sky and yells "Why me?" from the depths of her soul and waits for someone to come along with a solution to her problem. No growth can take place here—this is a stifling place of judging, blaming, and complaining.

When in this space, we say things like the following:

"I can't."

"Why me?"

"How could this be happening to me?"

"Who is going to save me?"

"How can I get someone to take care of me?"

Because the Damsel believes she is powerless, she never takes responsibility for her situation. Instead, she looks for someone to blame. I blamed God when I was in despair. You may do the same, or you may hold a variety of people at fault for your pain: your partner, your parents, your boss, your friends, your siblings.

As Damsels, we give away our power repeatedly—to the personal-development guru, the religious leader, the boyfriend, the boss—because we wholeheartedly believe the answer lies outside of ourselves. In our distress, we may even turn to manipulating others to get our needs met, rather than meeting those needs ourselves.

Alessandra's Story

Alessandra told me that her marriage worked perfectly, as long as her husband brought home the money and she looked good on his arm at social events. It had been a long time since they'd had any semblance of physical or emotional intimacy, and she was well aware of his numerous extramarital affairs. But she put up with his "vice" because they had children to care for, and she had no income of her own. Plus she did not want to work outside the home.

But she had grown tired of their arrangement. She felt she deserved a partner who was capable of giving her something deeper than what she was presently getting. For a long while all she wanted to talk about during our sessions was her husband—she blamed him for his lustful ways and for her discontent. But soon we started to talk about her father.

Alessandra's father was an emotionally distant man who'd left her mother and moved on with a new wife. Occasionally he sent money, but otherwise she'd had no contact with him. After he abandoned them, Alessandra and her family had lived in extreme poverty. Those extended family members who could worked night and day just to put food on the table, and there were no resources or time available for anything besides their basic needs. As a teenager, she hustled on the streets so that she could contribute to the household income. She never had the time to discover who she was, what she liked, what she wanted out of life. And emotional intimacy simply hadn't been part of the equation.

As she relayed the story of her childhood and her father, Alessandra realized that she had created a similar dynamic with her husband. When I asked her what emotional intimacy *felt* like, she had no clue, though she knew that she wanted it. None of her relationships ever went past a certain depth, including the one she had with herself. She realized it was the survivor in her that had gotten married for financial security.

She was ready to explore herself on a different level, as she now had the time and resources available to do so. After deep self-exploration, she started to be more authentically present with herself, and she finally felt confident enough to voice her feelings to her husband.

"I didn't know you were so unhappy," he told her. "I didn't think you cared, actually. You never acted like what I did one way or the other even mattered to you, and to be honest, I've been incredibly lonely."

When Alessandra allowed herself to seek connection with her husband and ask for the same in return, she discovered that all along he had wanted the same thing. He'd been looking for it elsewhere but had come up empty-handed. With much hard work, they were able to create a more loving, honest relationship.

The Superwoman

The Damsel lets herself off the hook and places unrealistic expectations on others, but the Superwoman does the opposite.

The Superwoman is caught up in the mindless pursuit of having it all, according to society's standards. She takes on the world, and she does so alone, even if she is in a relationship. She refuses support or help, either consciously or subconsciously. She juggles the career, the partner, the kids, the bills, the home, the groceries, the social life, the charity work, and on, and on, and on. And society endorses this! The Superwoman is talked about with statements like "Look how she has it all together" or "She can do anything and everything." Let's be honest, ladies. The action hero has nothing on her.

She juggles it all until something gives—and something always gives. A Superwoman lives in exhaustion for so long, she no longer recognizes it as such, and it simply becomes the normal state. She hasn't taken a day off for as long as she can remember, and she's replaced sleep with work. *Heck,* she thinks, *I can sleep when I'm dead.*

But one doesn't have to be in the workplace to be a Superwoman. Many homemakers feel the unrealistic burden of being the perfect mother, gourmet chef, local volunteer, and trophy wife. Their time is filled with checking off a never-ending to-do list. Though in a traditionally feminine role, this Superwoman still draws from overly masculine power to compete—to be the best, the most liked, the most efficient, the most nurturing, all while maintaining that youthful glow. She strives to prove she can do it all. The Superwoman's self-worth is so identified with what she can do that asking her to stop "doing" is the equivalent of death. She simply does not know who she is if she is not "doing."

You hear Superwomen say the following:

"I can do it all on my own."

"I don't need help."

"If you want it done right, you've got to do it yourself."

"Life is tough. Suck it up and get through it."

"I have to be strong. It's the only option."

"Weak women don't make it in this world."

"I have to act like a man to survive in this world."

"There's no time for self-care."

The option to say no doesn't even cross a Superwoman's mind. Allowing herself to receive support from those who care is a sign of weakness, so she dismisses this possibility without consideration because she would rather die trying than hurt her pride by accepting help.

Sabrina's Story

Sabrina was a beautiful eastern European woman with platinum-blond hair, a model's figure, and a wardrobe straight off the catwalk. Rarely did she not have a cigarette hanging from her lips, and she walked like she owned the world.

Sabrina came to me because she felt like her relationship was at a dead end. Her partner, Ivan, constantly accused her of being angry, while she'd had it with him behaving like a "two-year-old who refuses to take any responsibility." She found her anger justified, since she did everything—she was the primary breadwinner, and she took care of the kids, maintained the house, and supported both extended families financially, emotionally, and in any other way that was needed. Her husband, on the other hand, was rarely home and never spent time with the kids, and although he made a decent income, he was more than happy to be the absentee father, husband, brother, and son. He claimed he couldn't be around his wife's anger, while Sabrina retorted that that was just his excuse to be out and about all day (and all night) and not share the responsibility of the family. To her, Ivan was the typical male that "fucked off" just when he was needed. And to top it off, her eldest child had started to rebel, and she had no idea how to handle it.

When I brought up her husband's accusations about her anger, Alessandra exploded into a seething rage. Amid angry tears, she yelled about what an "asshole" her husband was for not being there for her, about how he was acting like a child and she didn't want another child—she wanted a partner. She questioned why she was even married if she had to endure the burden all on her own. She was on the verge of a physical breakdown, and I wasn't sure how long she could keep going.

"What happens when you ask for help?" I said. She reiterated that her husband wouldn't do anything—or couldn't do anything right. Eventually, she realized that even when Ivan agreed to help, she inevitably stepped in and did it herself because she didn't actually trust him. She saw how this undermined him and left him feeling powerless to shoulder any share of the burden. She was asking for support but didn't know how to receive it.

I asked her to step into the role of her husband. As Ivan, she felt hammered by expectations and saw Sabrina as a ticking time bomb that the slightest pressure would set off. For the first time, she could see why she might be difficult to be around. As we dug deeper, she revealed that her mom was also the quintessential Superwoman. She'd raised the kids and made the money—and then her husband had left her for another woman. With that as her model, Sabrina knew no other way to be. Throw in the pressure she felt to be thin (thus the excessive smoking) and fashionable, and she truly was a bomb about to explode.

Ivan wanted recognition and acceptance—recognition for his contributions to the family and acceptance of who he was. Both of which Sabrina, as a Superwoman, couldn't give herself, let alone someone else. She was so deeply embedded in this facade that she would have to relearn who she was without it so she could allow others to be who they really were, to support her when she needed it, and to love her for who she really was. Sure enough, as she let go of her impossible expectations, her partner started to step up and show up. And her relationship with her son, who needed a mother rather than a Superwoman, improved as well.

The Third Mind-Set—The Leader of Change

The Superwoman and Damsel paradigms are not always simple in real life. You may be behaving like a Superwoman in one area and a complete victim in another. For example, a woman could be a career Superwoman but an entirely disempowered Damsel in her relationship with her partner. Some women change from Damsel to Superwoman at the flip of a switch. If you go from "Please help me" to "To hell with you, I can do this by myself," you have jumped from one extreme to the other.

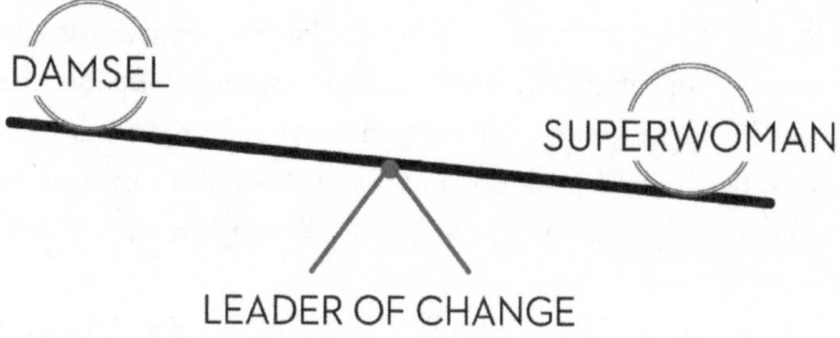

Figure 2.1: The Seesaw of Facades

If we are swinging between these two false choices, it is likely that we are moved by a voice that, more often than not, is the ego's voice, society's voice, peer pressure's voice, our parent's voice. But there is another voice. A deeper voice. A more powerful voice. A voice aligned with your soul's purpose that flows not from the throat but from the heart. The voice of your feminine potential. Therein lies the challenge—to listen to *that* voice.

Let's take a moment here to unpack the commonly held notion of what it means for us as women to be strong. Many women I've talked to associate strength with being a warrior—enduring pain with grace and dignity and a smile on one's face. But why do we need to endure pain in the first place? To me, there is greater strength in adapting to what life brings, rather than helplessly holding on to pain or waiting in full armor with fists ready for the next blow the universe delivers. To drop either of these extremes takes a great deal of courage. You have to be ready to face your own demons, to be comfortable being vulnerable and asking for help, and to allow yourself to be a bit of a mess—you will be a beautiful mess while doing it.

It's OK not to have everything together. Those perfect Hollywood moms we're meant to idolize have makeup artists, nannies, and a big behind-the-scenes team to create and uphold their facades for them. Surely not everyone wants these manufactured dreams: the bloated bank account, Brad Pitt hubby, mansion on four acres, and closet the size of Texas fully stocked with designer clothing.

Have you ever felt capable of changing the world and the world within, even if it was just for a moment? When you're in that space, you feel grounded, confident, and unafraid. You take responsibility for your life. You have control over your actions and reactions. This is the third mind-set, when you are thinking as a Leader of Change and acting in a way that reflects that. You thoughtfully choose your actions because you know who you are and why you are here.

Strong enough to listen, confident enough to contribute, you are devoted to bringing out the best in everyone, including yourself. You are comfortable with taking the lead as well as cooperating with others or learning from those with more experience or expertise. You take your time making up your own mind, focusing on clarity and what's truly important.

In this mind-set, you are clear on your priorities, and you have the ability to decide what and who takes precedent. You have a heartfelt interest in the growth and happiness of those around you, and you are able to nurture others and provide a community in which they feel like they belong. This ability to prioritize people over profits defines your relationship with money. The community's interests come first, though you don't have a problem with making money—because you know that money serves a greater good and allows you to impact more people.

In this mind-set, you do not need to submit to anyone, nor do you have the need to dominate. You are confident in your connectedness and, at the same time, complete within yourself.

To determine whether you are motivated by a Leader of Change mind-set, simply ask yourself, "Is my life a copy of someone else's dream, or is it an original of my own devising? Am I doing what external voices tell me to do, or am I following the guidance of my inner voice?" Ponder your authentic needs versus what you've been conditioned to believe you want. Because you won't get what you want until you know what you want. And you won't know what you want until you manifest the woman you are. Ladies, you *can* have it all. But first you must define what "having it all" means to you.

If you can do this, you will become your best self—the same person in public and in private. Living with integrity, you'll have no fear of someone finding out about some part of your life. The secrets will be revealed, the closets cleaned out, the leverage anyone might have had over you removed. Imagine the freedom that comes with living a life in absolute integrity. Nothing hanging over your head. No shadow hovering over your heart. You will be free to walk with your head high, with your back straight, without fear. You will no longer point the finger of blame at anyone, not even yourself. You can come down from your Damsel tower and put your Superwoman cape away. Because wouldn't you rather be *your* version of happy?

REFLECTION EXERCISES

When we ask disempowering questions of ourselves such as "Why am I so unhappy?" or "Why am I so lonely?" our minds might be filled with demeaning answers. We may hear ourselves say, "You don't deserve happiness!" or "No one could ever love you." However, when we ask empowering questions of ourselves, we will receive empowering answers.

- In which situations or relationships do you take on the role of Damsel?
- In which situations or relationships do you take on the role of Superwoman?
- What do you gain from playing each of these roles? What do you lose?
- What does "strong" mean to you?
- What obstacles might you face if you decide to become a Leader of Change?

Chapter Three

T = Take Ownership of Your Life

The Leader of Change Response to Life

Losing my baby knocked me to my emotional, physical, and spiritual knees. But not for long. As quickly as possible, I'd put my Superwoman mask back in place and ventured out into the world again. I walked through the streets of Dubai past other women dressed in a variety of ways, from form-hiding abayas to the Western styles worn by expatriates to some mix of the two, depending on each woman's cultural background. I always wore designer clothes and killer heels, so I appeared to be a highly successful, financially secure woman in charge of her own life. The truth was that my knees wobbled and my heart was heavy with self-doubt. The discrepancy between how I looked and how I felt haunted me. It motivated me to regain my sense of control at all costs, and I adamantly refused to let life whip me around according to its whims. I would not settle for anything but the best. The only problem was I did not know what "the best" looked like anymore, now that my spiritual and emotional life had been upended.

My confusion was not from lack of intellectual effort. I had plenty of academic accolades to my name and the training in rational thinking to go with them. Yet I was unable to answer the most pressing question of life, most simply stated: "How do I handle this terrible situation?"

Scholars can dissect and analyze indefinitely, but at the end of the day, who has the answers? There's a reason they say the longest journey you'll ever take is twelve inches, from the mind to the heart. And I was about to take my first step.

With lots of brainpower and nothing to show for it, I decided to expand my focus beyond intellectual concepts to more experiential modalities. I studied Reiki, ThetaHealing, the law of attraction, and quantum mechanics. I read the likes of Gregg Braden, Bruce Lipton, and others who attempted to merge the worlds of spirituality and science. Immersing myself in cutting-edge therapies, I participated in many forms of personal development and went on to become an integrated clinical hypnotherapist.

Still, the questions hounded me. Why had life dealt me this blow? Why was I not in control? Why weren't the skills and mindset that had worked for me in the past working for me now?

I had yet to learn that if you ask questions of the universe, it will answer you in good time. I was not quite prepared when the answer did come, unexpectedly and not at all in the way that I'd imagined.

In a specialized life-coach training workshop, I sat restlessly among my fellow trainees. The group split up into pairs to practice a coaching process. My partner, a woman I'd met in class but didn't know well, stepped into the coach's role, while I was the client.

"How are you feeling?" she asked.

"Stuck," I responded offhandedly.

"What does 'stuck' look like to you?"

I got off the chair and sat down on the carpeted floor. I put my arms across my chest and curled up into a tight ball in the fetal position. I found it hard to breathe.

And then it struck me like a thunderbolt.

I was Lia—the daughter I'd lost—paralyzed in my womb. And Lia was a reflection of me. She mirrored my "stuckness." My paralysis.

As I lay sobbing on the floor, the tears stinging my eyes, I realized my fourteen-week-old daughter would teach me one of my most profound life lessons: our lives are reflections of ourselves.

I was not physically paralyzed, but life wasn't flowing through me emotionally and relationally. I had been unable to admit to the world, let alone to myself, what I was feeling. I was paralyzed by my own facade of strength. My veneer was my greatest barrier to life.

When the power of my realization subsided, I silently got to my feet. I made the decision that I would hide no longer. I didn't know what I was hiding. Or what I was hiding from. But I didn't need to have all those answers to take my next step. I was no longer trying to find someone to blame—neither myself nor anyone else. There *was* no one to blame—all that was left was for me to take responsibility for my own life and step into my immense personal power.

Your Reality Is of Your Own Making

The only way to find peace is through taking ownership of your own life. The phrase "taking ownership" has been used to convey many things—none of which are what I mean by "taking ownership." So let me start by identifying what I don't mean. Let's consider what the Damsel and the Superwoman would do.

The Damsel

The Damsel refuses to take ownership of herself and her life. Trapped in a high tower like Rapunzel or knocked out cold like Snow White, she waits for other people to rescue her, taking no action on her own behalf. How could she? She doesn't even know what she needs, or if she does, she doesn't know how to say it. Even if she wanted to alter something, it's likely that she'd just be spinning her wheels, since she'd rather not face the issue and therefore doesn't accurately grasp the problem. She sees herself as powerless, and when no one comes to save her, or those who do fall short of her expectations, she sits around and complains and blames. The Damsel simply waits, agonizing over unfulfilled dreams, seething with rage and disappointment when the knights don't arrive in full armor atop their white steeds.

The Superwoman

The Superwoman, on the other hand, takes on too much responsibility. Along with her cape she carries the weight of the world on her shoulders, and her shoulders alone, unable to share the load with anyone else. The Superwoman is equally misguided about what her problem is. A Superwoman thinks she needs to manage her time better so she can get more done. She makes lists and gleefully checks off each task as she buzzes frantically through her life. Her time for sleep is short so she can do more in a day, and her rest is disrupted by anxious dreams. She wakes up each morning already overwhelmed by the mountain of work in front of her, others' needs she feels compelled to meet, and the deadlines that loom on the horizon. She will bulldoze her way through her life, rolling over whatever crosses her path, in order to get everything done.

"OK!" you might be saying. "I get your point. I want to break free of this false dichotomy . . . but how? How do I climb out of my tower or drop my cape to the floor? It's all I know."

Well, I'm glad you asked. Because the answer is simple: *take ownership of what you have created.*

That statement might sting a bit or maybe even infuriate you. I realize it is likely that you picked up this book because you are struggling with a difficult or agonizing issue, and the last thing you want to hear is that you are the one who created it.

Perhaps you think difficult things happen to you because of God's whimsy, because of bad luck, or because you somehow deserve them. As a result, you are like a little child at the beach, being relentlessly knocked over by the waves. You barely stand up before the next one hits, throwing you headfirst into the froth and sand. When you manage to scramble to your feet, you lock your knees in defiance. Then the next one hits, and once again you are thrashing under the water.

But once you realize that the waves are here to teach you, not to traumatize you, your interpretation and experience of life can be transformed. No one is trying to conquer you; life is not here to harm you. Rather than lock your knees, you can move with the ebb and flow of the water. When the waves suck the sand out from under your feet, you can dive, patiently waiting until the right moment to find new footing.

The events that come into your life are meant to teach you something new, something significant and life changing that will make you healthier and stronger, a better friend and family member. When you alter the way you interpret these events, you stop asking "Why me?" and start asking "What is this here to teach me?"

When we view our circumstances from this point of view, the fear of failure dissipates. The desire to be perfect diminishes. It becomes much easier to be kind to ourselves when we're not trying to earn an A or a gold star in every situation. We relax instead of resisting and are open to new ideas instead of arguing for unexamined beliefs. If you don't understand the lesson the first time around, you can be certain the situation will return to give you another chance. It's not a pass-or-fail test—it's a learning curve. There's no pressure. Just compassion.

Once I learned that Lia's paralysis was a reflection of my paralysis, I understood my entire life as a reflection of myself. That is an extremely powerful place to be. I was learning how to take ownership of my own life and accept every situation, painful or pleasant, as the gift that it was—an opportunity for learning, a reflection of an unseen and disavowed part of me that I needed to heal.

We have no control over the events that take place in our lives, and we don't have the power to change our partners, friends, family members, or anyone else. While we are responsible for nurturing, protecting, and parenting our children, ultimately they must make their own decisions. You can't force your boss or best friend to be kind and supportive, so don't take responsibility for his or her actions, or waste time trying to get the response you desire rather than doing what you think is right. You have power over one and only one person, and that is you.

You get to choose how you respond to every experience. And ultimately, it is your response that determines the outcome. Taking ownership of yourself is being able to recognize your own distress, your own needs, your own goals, and then acting on behalf of yourself. You are only responsible for what you are able to change.

Examine Your Inner Reality

Every tragedy carries an opportunity for transformation; every uncomfortable situation, the seed of change. Our greatest teachers are those we perceive to have wronged us. It is precisely these people whom we should be grateful for, because we learn more about ourselves when we face adversity.

Uncomfortable situations are uncomfortable because they mirror our internal reality. We are seeing something about ourselves we do not want to see. To be the change the world so desperately needs, we have to be willing to face these parts of ourselves. Not only do we need to face them, but we need to shine a light on them to examine them from all angles.

Listen to Your Pain

Just as physical pain lets us know something needs to change, emotional pain does the same. And believe it or not, listening to what our emotions are trying to tell us decreases pain in the long run.

Let's say, for example, you are being cheated on. Many women have suffered betrayal of one kind or another. What would happen if you listened to your pain, if you asked it some tough questions? In this case, you might ask, "Where in my life am I cheating myself? How am I cheating someone else?" If someone is showing you disrespect, you could ask, "How am I being disrespectful to others? Where am I lacking in self-respect?"

You might then say to me, "Oh, this is too hard. I don't want to listen to these parts of myself." I understand. But trying to sidestep a problem will not make it go away. Instead it will come up again and again. We'll date the same kind of person over and over (same drama, different face) or get into the same Facebook argument for the umpteenth time or find ourselves alone and lonely for fourteen Saturday nights in a row.

That pain is part of an unhealthy pattern, an indication we're not learning something. It is necessary to break the pattern in order to grow.

Own What Is Yours

When we are unable to take ownership of our own demons, we project them onto others. Triggers are the signal that it's time to examine our own baggage—if someone's actions upset you and draw a reaction out of you, it is as though that person is holding up a mirror to something inside you. Seeing people through the lens of our unhealed baggage is seeing them not for who they truly are but who *we* truly are.

You can see this in the news any day of the week. We have the descendants of immigrants trying to build walls to keep newer immigrants out, and groups maintaining blood feuds for centuries after the initial conflict. We have countries and religious leaders labeling one another as extremists or aggressors when they are doing the same thing, perhaps in a different form. These are obvious examples of the never-ending ping-pong game of projections.

We must let go of our projections to correct the trajectory of the planet. Allowing people to be who they truly are versus who we choose to see them as is what I'd call real freedom. I must honor who you really are, and you must honor who I really am—then the unique gifts we have can be expressed.

Michelle's Story

Michelle had lost her job. Again. She'd scheduled her first session with me for a time right before a job interview, hoping to "get it all sorted out" beforehand. Rushing into my office five minutes late, she threw her brown leather bag on the floor and sat heavily on the chair. She was dressed just as you'd expect for an accountant—sensible black shoes, a knee-length black skirt, light-blue button-up shirt, her hair pulled back in a smart bun.

After Michelle told me about her career situation, I asked her what had happened in her last job.

"My ex-boss is an absolute idiot," she said, rolling her eyes. She then went on to relay the exact dimensions of his idiocy in great length. After a few minutes, I gently cut her off.

"You mentioned that this is the fourth job you've had in the last four years. What happened at the job before that?"

"That boss was totally corrupt." Again, Michelle began to describe in detail just how corrupt he was. Again, I gently interrupted.

"And the one before that?"

"Jerk. He couldn't handle having an employee smarter than him."

"And the one before that?"

"You are not going to believe just how—" She stopped. Her eyes widened. I could see the moment of realization in the expression on her face.

"Do you see a pattern?" I asked, keeping my voice soft.

Over the course of six months of weekly sessions, Michelle revealed a pattern that had plagued her all her life. Her preschool teachers had told her parents that she might be better served staying home. She'd switched schools three times, been kicked off the track team, and been asked to leave the debate club because she couldn't maintain a professional demeanor. Her romantic relationships usually didn't last long, and the one or two that had had been tumultuous, to say the least. She'd lost every job she'd had, from babysitting to grocery clerking to legal assisting.

"It's *me*," she said one day, tears filling her eyes.

After that, we spent a long time talking about her pain. Her anger was fiery and obvious, the most superficial layer of feeling, and she expressed it often and fully in her life. But underneath that were shame and sadness, loneliness and despair.

"What is this pain trying to tell you?" I asked over and over.

For the next few months, I tried to nudge Michelle toward observing her own behavior. When she talked about how stupid her boss was, I asked her about *her* behavior in the situation. When she complained about the incompetence of her best friend, I asked her about *her* behavior in the situation. When she told me that everyone was out to get her, I asked her about *her* behavior.

This was not a comfortable process. Sometimes she'd lash out at me, tell me that these sessions were pointless or that I didn't know what I was doing. One day, she began to act out her frustration, yelling and stomping her feet. I could barely get a word in edgewise.

"So this is what it's like to be on the receiving end of your anger," I finally managed to say. "I'm not going to argue with you, you know."

She paused, obviously taken aback. "Why not?" she said.

"I'm not the one you're angry with."

Learning comes through first facing a dynamic within yourself. The external situation is a reflection of this dynamic, and it points you toward what needs resolution within. If you lose your job over and over again, it's probably a good idea to stop and consider your own behavior as well as your internal processes. If you are being bullied, you have to look at both the bully and the dynamic *within yourself.* If you are being cheated on, lied to, disrespected, or demeaned, then this inner dynamic needs to be addressed before you can create change on the outside.

The framework below allows us to view situations that arise in everyday life from different perspectives. The external situation encompasses a particular trigger, and the potential responses of the Damsel, the Superwoman, and the Leader of Change follow.

> External situation: *My boss is constantly criticizing me.*
>
> Damsel response: *I am worth nothing.*
>
> Superwoman response: *To hell with all of you. I'll show you!*

Leader of Change response: *How am I criticizing myself? How am I critical of others?*

External situation: *My partner is cheating on me.*

Damsel response: *How could he do this to me?*

Superwoman response: *How dare he!*

Leader of Change response: *How am I cheating myself? How am I cheating others?*

External situation: *My peers are fat shaming me.*

Damsel response: *Oh no, I look horrible!*

Superwoman response: *I don't give a damn what they think.*

Leader of Change response: *In what ways do I feel ashamed of my own body?*

The Vital Importance of Self-Love

The Leader of Change does not give up her power, nor does she take on too much. Instead, she focuses her energy on the part of her that is contributing to the creation of the situation and how to change the only thing she can—herself.

Although unhealed issues can come in many forms, the good news is that one thing can resolve the majority of them: self-love.

Self-love is necessary to make illuminating our darkest corners bearable—it allows us to own our lives gently and without blame. Self-love elevates your life—it determines whom you attract and shows them how you want to be treated, just by the way you carry yourself. Don't focus on setting boundaries or finding the right mate; rather, focus on your inner state and let the externals fall into place.

When we accept the many aspects of who we are and bring them out into the open, when we bring light into our own darkness, we begin to strut into our own power, back into our original essence instead of the shape the world told us to be.

Self-love is an art form and an act of rebellion. You have to dedicate yourself to it; you have to overcome obstacles in order to master it. The current world paradigm is one of self-loathing. If you practice self-love, you will be going against the trend, and initially it will take all your might to stay on course. But it gets easier.

Self-love is fundamental to steering the growth of humanity in the right direction. An individual who treats herself with kindness has a greater capacity to treat others with kindness. Countries that value their citizens as individuals worthy of care and compassion are more likely to view the citizens of other countries from that same loving perspective.

Love yourself so that you can more fully love others.

Let us look at the previous examples again. In the situation with the critical boss, the question you would ask yourself is, "How can I love the part of me that is critical?" With a cheating partner, the question would be "How can I love the part of me that cheats or has been cheated?" In the last example, about the fat-shaming peers, you would ask, "How can I bring more love to how I think about and treat my body?"

You can be a better version of yourself and open yourself up to limitless possibilities by using whatever situation you are facing as a stepping stone for growth. Evaluating a challenge while it is happening can be difficult—usually you'll have trouble seeing it clearly until you view it in hindsight. But looking at it now, while it hurts, might allow you to see outside your tunnel vision and view the situation in a new way.

Nothing is happening *to* you but rather *for* you, for your growth.

REFLECTION EXERCISES

Describe a situation that you are currently struggling with. Take time to add detail to your description of the events involved, as well as the feelings this experience triggered in you. Then answer these questions:

- Do you tend to blame yourself or blame your circumstances? How might this tendency serve you and harm you?
- What unhealed part of you are you having difficulty facing? What disowned part of you do you need to acknowledge?
- What is that unhealed part of you trying to convey? What is it that you don't want to hear?
- What do you need to take ownership of? What in this situation is internal, and what is external? What do you have the power to control, and what belongs to someone else?
- How can you build or maintain self-love, even when things are difficult?

Chapter Four

R = Reconnect with Your Body

The Devastating Disconnection from Our Bodies

There I was, sitting in a personal-development workshop crammed full of people. The energy was dense. The smell of sweat hovered in the air. We were four days in, and I didn't feel any better.

I was resentful as we broke into pairs for another dreaded exercise. I turned to the man sitting next to me. He wore a black turban to represent his religion and had gentle eyes and a warm smile. *Run, Samar, run,* I thought as every molecule in my body tried to inch toward the door.

The man leaned toward me and placed my hands in his. "Whom would you like to forgive?" he asked.

"No one. I'm good." My regular tough-woman attitude kicked in, and I was damn proud of it.

"Really? No one?"

"Nope, not a soul."

He paused and looked into my eyes. He said gently, "Someone from your childhood, perhaps?" His words shuddered through my body.

How could he have known? The bastard. I had attended this workshop with hopes of finding some answers to the questions that continued to nag at me. But when this man opened the door for me, instead of feeling relieved, I became enraged. Just because I'd chosen to be there didn't make him any less of a bastard to me at that moment.

"I was abused at the age of three." The words sputtered out of my mouth before any of my defense mechanisms could kick in. Tears came out so hard and fast I was gasping for breath within a minute. A meltdown in public. Tough women don't cry in front of others. Hell, they don't cry at all.

I held my face in my hands as the tears streamed down. In my mind's eye, I could see it all. Experience it all again. There in the past I cried, but no one heard my three-year-old calls for help. In front of me was a wooden door, with dark-blue tiled walls on either side. The dim light couldn't hide the two monsters that stood between me and my freedom.

When I was three, I was locked in a school bathroom by two teen bullies. They put sand in my eyes. They took my panties off and flushed them down the toilet. They beat me relentlessly. They did things I still struggle to put into words. For weeks this was my daily nightmare. Most three-year-olds skip along to the playground during the recess after lunch. I was dragged to the bathroom every single day and endured abuse that bordered on torture.

Every day, the teen girls dumped me outside the bathroom when recess was over, and I would make my way back to class, crying. My teacher didn't have a clue as to what was happening.

Life was a blur from one lunchtime to another. The teenagers came back to class to pick me up. I cowered behind my teacher at her desk, begging her not to let them take me.

"Run along and play with your friends, Samar," she remarked as she continued to grade papers. She didn't even turn to look at me as, for the umpteenth time, they came to take me away. I didn't have the vocabulary to explain what was happening.

One day, I came home with a swollen lip. My father noticed my injury and immediately called the school. We all met with the school supervisor. They asked me who had done this to me, and I identified the girls. The scope of what they'd done to me did not come to light. The adults thought that the teens had hit me once and now the ordeal was resolved. The two girls were suspended from school. I never saw them again.

I was awakened from these dark memories by cheers and applause. I blinked at the workshop group through my tears.

"Good on you! You finally got her to cry," yelled a male voice from the corner.

"It's about time, honestly," another participant said as she put her arm around me. The whole class had seen through my Superwoman facade from the moment I walked in. And they were all secretly rooting for the moment I would drop the act. My tough-woman ego was a tad bit bruised (*Really? They can see through me?*), but I was overwhelmed by the love that they gave me—people I barely knew but who somehow knew me better than most. For the first time in a long time, I felt safe. For the first time in a long time, I let go.

A year later, I sat with an acquaintance who was practicing to be a life coach. We had been talking and talking and talking, but we weren't making much progress.

Since we had hit a dead end, she had the idea of blindfolding me to see whether limiting one of my senses would open things up. I agreed, thinking nothing much would come of it.

The scarf tied in place, I felt calm at first. The elimination of my sense of sight put me in immediate contact with my body.

"What's happening?" she asked.

"There's something in front of me," I said, my voice quivering.

"What is it?"

"A block. It won't let me move."

She remained silent while I continued to decipher what was going on. With great difficulty, I got to my feet but could move no farther. I called for her to support me, but she didn't budge.

The blockage was a darkness at first. Then it came into focus. "It's a door," I said. In my mind, I saw that wooden door in front of me. It was the bathroom door that had been too large and heavy for me to open when I was trapped by those cruel teenagers. My thirty-three-year-old armor dropped, and I was a broken child again. I was stripped bare of dignity, trust, worthiness—everything that makes us human.

"What door?" she asked. I couldn't speak. I was unsure of what to do, and my words failed me—just as they had then. She helped me sit down and stroked my hair as I lay there in my brokenness.

The understanding poured over me like a wave. When I was three, I didn't have the capacity to fight back. The Superwoman I had become was a result of the broken child within that I had been so desperate to protect. The veneer—beautiful and shining and hard—had kept everything out, both good and bad. I didn't believe in asking for help, because when I had, I hadn't received any. I didn't trust the world, because how could I? My sense of self had been obliterated before it'd had a chance to blossom.

And because of the abuse, I had become cut off from my body.

There's a Reason

Few—if any—of us make a conscious decision to abandon our physical selves. It is a decision our unconscious minds make in the face of overwhelming terror and a sense of helplessness.

The mind is hardwired to protect us and keep us alive,[6] even if that means splitting from the body.[7] As a result of this split, we live in our heads, out of touch with our true emotions, ignoring signals of distress, unable to truly touch other human beings on a deep level. The Damsel tells herself she's the victim and teaches her body that there is something big and bad out there that is coming to get her. The Superwoman insists that she cannot be defeated, thereby putting her body into combat mode. Both mind-sets shout, "We are at war!"

As a consequence, our bodies are perpetually on high alert, constantly preparing for war. And when we prepare for war, we attract conflict within and without. It is present even in our language: we "battle" a chronic disease or have "defeated" a life-threatening illness like cancer. We "fight" for a promotion at work, "surrender" our lives to a relationship, or "struggle" with our weight.

If you are living in your body as though it were a war zone, there's a reason. Probably more than one. No one cuts herself off from intimacy and personal power without strong motivation.

---

6 "Stress Basics," Mayo Clinic, last modified March 31, 2017, http://www.mayoclinic.org/healthy-lifestyle/stress-management/basics/stress-basics/hlv-20049495.

7 George Simon, "Understanding 'Splitting' as a Psychological Term," Counselling Resource, October 28, 2008, http://counsellingresource.com/features/2008/10/28/splitting-as-psychological-term/.

The challenge for us is to discover the reason or reasons—because most of us honestly don't know why we do what we do. We must dig deeper and find out *why*. The step you took toward ownership in the last chapter is necessary in the art of self-awareness. None of us have the power to handle what is not our responsibility. But you now know that you are strong enough to carry what *is* your responsibility. With that awareness and confidence, it's time to go deeper and ask yourself, "What is the reason I am hiding?"

Physical Trauma

Survival is our most basic instinct. When something hurts, we pull away. If something is dangerous, we fight or flee.

But what do we do when we are unable to get away from the pain? How do we find a sense of safety when we're too powerless to fight or too small to flee? This is where our minds kick in and do the best they can by removing our sense of consciousness from the source of pain. Using a primitive yet effective mechanism, we cut ourselves off not only from the abuse but from the point in our bodies where we experience the pain.[8]

Often we punish our bodies for feeling pain, rather than recognize the thing—or person—that inflicted the pain. The war raging inside can stay inside for only so long. As long as our minds and our bodies are in conflict, our outer world will be too.

---

8 Robin Roberts, "The Mind-Body Connection," Mind-Body Psychotherapy, accessed April 11, 2017, https://www.mindbodypsychotherapy.net/mbconnection.htm.

Laila's Story

Laila and her husband's relationship was at a breaking point. The soft-spoken young woman arrived at my office with a beautiful veil covering her hair, the latest sunglasses perched on her nose, and a designer handbag on her arm. She described, in casual English dotted with Arabic slang, how the connection just wasn't there anymore. Her husband, Abdullah, seemed scared of her, and she was utterly baffled as to why.

Over the course of a few sessions, she recounted the story of her mother's childhood abuse at the hands of a relative. Laila soon realized that her mother had never been fully physically present in her body, and their relationship had always been cold, lacking in maternal warmth and caring. Laila had internalized this model as the only way to stay safe and had unintentionally re-created that style of relationship with her husband.

I encouraged Laila to reconnect with her body, but for a long time she simply couldn't access her physical being. When she finally did, rage was the first sensation to fill her consciousness. The anger that she'd always had but had never been able to express was finally released, and it erupted violently. Once she calmed down, Laila was able to articulate that the locus of her anger was, unsurprisingly, her mother and their absence of connection. After intense processing and forgiveness work, Laila came to understand that her husband had sensed and been afraid of this underlying fury all along.

External situation: *My husband is afraid of me.*

Damsel response: *I have no idea why and no way to figure it out.*

Superwoman response: *He's being such a baby!*

Leader of Change response:

Self-reflection: What am I afraid of? How is that fear manifesting itself in the world?

Self-love: How can I nurture myself so that I can face this fear?

Neglect

I have worked with many women who are cut off from their bodies and their potential, despite never having experienced physical violation. Emotional neglect can be terribly painful, even though there are no visible bruises or scars. When our need for emotional nurturing is not met, we feel overlooked, as if our existence doesn't matter. Emotional neglect has the same effect on our brains as physical pain does.[9]

A lack of nurturing is a predominant theme among my clients. If we don't experience nurturing as a child—a parent who is fully present, a caregiver who gives us loving embraces, a sense of being seen and heard—we grow up to be adults who seek this feeling elsewhere, through others, without knowing how to provide it for

9 Alan Fogel, "Emotional and Physical Pain Activate Similar Brain Regions," *Psychology Today*, April 19, 2012, https://www.psychologytoday.com/blog/body-sense/201204/emotional-and-physical-pain-activate-similar-brain-regions.

ourselves. In fact, research suggests that children who have been nurtured by their mothers have hippocampi—a region of the brain associated with learning, memory, and stress response—that are 10 percent larger than those who did not receive nurturing.[10]

Anika's Story

Anika was frustrated by her pattern of dating, which she described as being "stuck in a loop." She seemed to attract men she perceived to be too feminine—passive, indecisive, shy—who relied on her to perform what she thought of as the masculine role. She felt like the man in these relationships, since she always had the more prestigious career, the higher income, the well-networked social life. She was the ultimate Superwoman and couldn't find a Superman to match.

Soon the dynamic of her parents' marriage became the focus of our discussion. Anika described her mother as "insignificant" and "unseen," her father as "detached" and "disdainful." Her mother came from a culture in which female feticide was commonplace and the value of a boy's life far outweighed that of a girl's. She ignored Anika, instead focusing on her son, Arjun, perhaps compensating for her husband's neglect by lavishing extra attention on the only other male family member.

In the midst of our exploration, Anika stumbled upon pent-up feelings concerning emotional neglect. She had built her life around

10 Joseph Castro, "How a Mother's Love Changes a Child's Brain," Live Science, January 30, 2012, http://www.livescience.com/18196-maternal-support-child-brain.html.

acting "like a boy" in hopes of getting her parents' attention and validation. So she acted like a boy in her relationships too.

She also realized that she'd sacrificed her true calling to do what she thought her parents wanted her to do. "How dare they!" she shouted. "How could they? . . . Why me?" I pointed out that she was angry at her parents for neglecting her, when she, in turn, had neglected her true self. She was the one who had made the choice to forego her calling.

Anika left determined to shape her future differently—starting with a little self-love, care, and tenderness.

> External situation: *I date the same type of person over and over again—and he tends to be passive, indecisive, and shy.*
>
> Damsel response: *There are no decent men out there.*
>
> Superwoman response: *No man is ever going to be able to keep up with me!*
>
> Leader of Change response:
>
> *Self-reflection: What in me is passive, indecisive, and shy? Where am I out of balance?*
>
> *Self-love: How can I love this part of myself that's been neglected?*

Shame

Women are subjected to a host of demeaning and disempowering messages in the media and in society at large. One thing we women have in common is that we have all been told to doubt ourselves and to hate our bodies.

Let's be honest about this. There are many voices that harass us. No matter what culture you were raised in or how cosmopolitan your upbringing may have been, all societies communicate anti-women messages.

It starts on the playground, where we mock one another, give demeaning nicknames, or bully one another for our physical appearances. This doesn't stop when we grow up; it just changes forms or becomes more subtle. The world economy needs us to feel shame about our bodies so that we will buy products and services—not only ones that meet real needs but also those that are created by advertisers. If we are convinced that we are less than and flawed, lovable only when wearing the right clothes on the right body, not a hair out of place and lipstick perfectly applied, we will spend our money. Because of these damaging influences, we learn to feel deeply ashamed about who we are and about our bodies, and many of us even develop serious body-related issues, such as emotional eating, over- or under-exercising, or obsessive shopping for the next outfit that will finally cover the body hatred buried inside. We might even say yes when we mean no, or cover a bruise instead of calling the police.

Many of us who were raised in conservative environments were taught to cover ourselves at all times. If a boy or man even looks at us, we believe it is our fault and that we should feel ashamed. In many cultures, women are objectified, and *our* desires do not matter. In fact, a woman is not supposed to even have any desires—rather, she is the passive receptacle of the desires of others. If a woman owns her sexuality in even the slightest way, she risks being labeled a "whore."

This puts women throughout the world in a terrible bind. When neither a woman's agency nor her body is respected, violence against her becomes acceptable, even the norm. Gang rapes are all too rampant, and "honor killings" in the East are the twisted way in which a victim's family seeks "justice"—by murdering the girl or woman for bringing "dishonor" to her family, rather than taking a deep look at the fundamental values of the society in which this occurs.

According to a 2014 article in the *Washington Post*, in India incidents of rape have increased by 900 percent in the last four decades, while less than 10 percent of these crimes are reported, likely because the victims fear punishment from their families or communities.[11] Honor killings in Pakistan are also on the rise, with 1,100 women killed in 2015.[12]

In the United States, the Obama administration implemented new policies meant to create awareness about and eradicate sexual

11 Terrence McCoy, "India's Gang Rapes—and the Failure to Stop Them," *Washington Post,* May 30, 2014, https://www.washingtonpost.com/news/morning-mix/wp/2014/05/30/indias-culture-of-gang-rape-and-the-failure-to-stop-it/?utm_term=.0b01b5b78aff.

12 "Pakistan Honour Killings on the Rise, Report Reveals," BBC News, April 1, 2016, http://www.bbc.com/news/world-asia-35943732.

assault,[13] particularly on college campuses, but the staying power of these measures will be tested as the political season changes.

Across the globe sexual assault is commonplace, and in countries where reporting these crimes is even an option, often the authorities and the media are all too quick to blame the victim for being in the wrong place or wearing the wrong clothing or consuming alcohol, as though that were somehow an invitation for violation.[14]

Some of us live in environments that are safe enough for us to explore our sexuality and to report crimes without fear, sure that we will get the support we need. But for many of us, even having this conversation can put our very lives at stake. The question remains: How can we embrace our sexuality and retain our humanity, our safety, our freedom?

Linda's Story

Linda was exhausted. Tired in her body, to the point of barely being able to get out of bed, and tired in her heart. Every time she arrived for her appointment, I'd watch her movements—it seemed as though she had to drag herself through the room to the chair,

13 Juliet Eilperin, "Biden and Obama Rewrite the Rulebook on College Sexual Assaults," *Washington Post*, July 3, 2016, https://www.washingtonpost.com/politics/biden-and-obama-rewrite-the-rulebook-on-college-sexual-assaults/2016/07/03/0773302e-3654-11e6-a254-2b336e293a3c_story.html?utm_term=.cd5bb851182a.

14 James Palmer, "Victim Blaming Worsens Harm Done by Rape," Global Times, March 8, 2015, http://www.globaltimes.cn/content/910835.shtml.

that she was more collapsing than sitting down. Her undereye circles were so dark they looked like bruises, and she spoke slowly, like someone trying but failing to wake up.

At first, Linda wanted to talk about her love life. She felt like she was always attracting the wrong types of men. Either they were interested in only a one-night stand, or they were "boring," looking for a wife. And they all tended to disappear in the blink of an eye.

As we ventured into Linda's inner world, we discovered her intense shame about having any form of sexual desire. This was no great surprise, given her conservative upbringing in which a promiscuous woman—the femme fatale—was one with any form of sexual yearning and was akin to the devil. On the other hand, the virginal woman, devoid of any form of sexual desire, was lauded.

Finally, after many months of building trust, I discovered that there was more to her story. Linda was the second of three sisters, and though she described them as her "best friends," she also said, "Sometimes they give me a headache." Her older sister, Hanna, had married and had children early, and despite the fact that Hanna generally had a sunny disposition, Linda believed that her sister was unhappy within the parameters of her role. Plus, Hanna's husband was the strong and silent type, a dependable provider but not the most connected or emotionally available companion.

The youngest of the three, Sophia, had seen Hanna's example and decided to wait and build her career before settling down. She was the bright light of the family—until the day that she was sexually assaulted on the way home from work. Out of intense shame and fear of being blamed, she did not report the incident. She dared not tell her parents out of fear of what they might think, and confided only in Linda about what had happened. Sophia had been a shadow of her former self ever since.

Not only was Linda exhausted by the responsibility of taking care of her sisters, but she was drained by the energy she had to expend managing her own confusion, anger, and fear. She was exhausted by having to live in a world where violence against women is commonplace, by having to work so hard to strike a balance between being accomplished yet deferential, hardworking yet meek, with the threat of punishment for simply being a woman always present.

Her older sister had taken the safe path and found herself lonely and stifled, while her younger sister had chosen a bumpier road and been hurt by a stranger and felt abandoned by those who were meant to protect her. Linda was subconsciously trying to decide between two seemingly unworkable choices—with pain as the result of whichever she chose.

In doing so, she was attracting men with the two energies that resided within her. The more femme-fatale energy attracted the one-night-stand types, while the more virginal energy attracted the "I want to get married right now" types. Meanwhile, the femme fatale hated the monogamous men, while the virgin hated the one-night-stand guys—and everyone she dated ended up getting confused by her mixed signals.

Underlying it all were her deep-rooted shame and feelings of helplessness as a woman within her society—feelings that we worked to uncover and process. Over time, Linda was better able to release her repressed sexual energy into forms of creative expression that she was comfortable with and that her religion would permit. Slowly, because she was no longer having to expend so much energy controlling her own fears and desires, she regained her lost vitality. And she was able to take steps to help her sisters as best she could, while at the same time maintaining enough energy to take care of herself.

External situation: *I'm exhausted by having to live with oppression.*

Damsel response: *I just can't handle this.*

Superwoman response: *I'm going to power on.*

Leader of Change response:

Self-reflection: How am I oppressing myself? How am I expressing that oppression? How am I mishandling the energy it takes to manage my life?

Self-love: We live in a world where being born a woman comes with a certain kind of danger. How can I keep myself safe but at the same time harness my power?

The Condemnation of Emotion

We are told from our earliest years that expressing certain emotions is unacceptable. And frequently, those restrictions are assigned by gender.

"Boys don't cry!"
"Girls don't get mad!"
"Don't talk back!"

"Quit being such a baby!"

Heaven forbid that a man should express softness or vulnerability, and woe to the woman who expresses anger or frustration. And it would be quite uncouth to express any emotion with intensity! It's OK to smile, but don't be extremely happy. Don't show how proud you are of yourself when you achieve a goal—humility is much more attractive.

The condemnation of emotion forces us to flee from our bodies—where we experience the physical sensation of emotion—and into our heads. We learn to choose our words carefully and keep our faces frozen. The truth is, the richness of life lies in the diversity of our emotions. When we don't feel, we don't live.

Emma's Story

Emma was at her wits' end over her five-year-old son's tantrums and outbursts of aggression, and her relationship with her husband was so tumultuous that they seemed to be on the verge of divorce. Their marriage was going through a communication breakdown—although they were fighting, what really needed to be said was not being said.

Emma told me that she'd had a strict upbringing. Her father worked in the military, and he'd applied the same militant thinking to raising his children. In her family, emotions were forbidden, and everyone was expected to soldier through no matter what. Her mother, a homemaker, worked to make sure that everything was perfect and that no one rocked the boat (emotions had no place on the boat). As an adult, Emma didn't have a deep connection to her parents, since she didn't feel she could truly share what was going on in her life.

She realized how she was carrying on the less-than-communicative dynamic with her husband. Not only was she afraid to say what she wanted, but she wasn't sure what she was feeling. Deeper into our exploration, she related how the internalization of her emotions had created a wall that blocked everything—her husband and son included. As she committed to learning how to express her emotions on a daily basis, be it to herself or to those around her, she started to uncover how isolated her young son felt outside the wall she had built. He was lashing out at the wall, because he was desperate to feel connected to his mother. The more she came into her body and allowed herself to feel, the deeper the bond between them became. Sharing their feelings formed a bridge between them.

External situation: *My family is failing at communication.*

Damsel response: *My husband will never understand me.*

Superwoman response: *I just have to soldier on.*

Leader of Change response:

Self-reflection: What within myself do I not understand? Where in my life am I incurious?

Self-love: Can I love whatever is revealed if I decide to investigate?

The Power of Being Present in Your Body

When you were born, you were fully connected with your body. There was no sense of mind and body being separate. You were you—authentic, complete, connected, and ready to explore.[15]

All women are born with an innate wisdom, and our bodies are a vehicle for that essential intelligence. The problem is, with social training and trauma, we forget about the body's sacred wisdom, and we end up storing toxic emotions as a result.

Leaders of Change, no matter what we suffered after we emerged from the womb, have to rebuild that connection between mind and body. It's a process—as we take more responsibility for ourselves, we become more connected. Your ability to strut is in direct proportion to how reconciled you are with your body. Your body is waiting for you, ready to tell you so much about who you are and who you are meant to be.

Embrace Imperfection

I spent a lifetime acquiring degrees, polishing my "I'm so perfect" demeanor to become precociously successful. Communicating what was going on inside me was pointless, since I believed that there was no one to listen. I spent a lifetime being afraid of touch and being afraid to trust. I pushed any form of nurturance away.

It's a paradox, really. To step into our abilities as Leaders of Change, we need to surrender our false sense of weakness or strength. Damsels doubt their ability to care for themselves, and

---

15 Michael Eisen, "Don't Suppress, Express!," Huffington Post, December 23, 2012, http://www.huffingtonpost.com/michaeleisen/men-expressing-self_b_1961990.html.

Superwomen want to be strong at all costs. There is a difference between acting as if you are invincible and owning your own power, or between acting helpless and allowing yourself to be vulnerable. Regardless of which facade you hide behind, dropping it takes a tremendous amount of courage. You have to be ready to face yourself, to tolerate being vulnerable and asking for the right kind of help while doing it.

Let me tell you from firsthand experience—you will survive even if you're not perfect. You know how I know this? Because you and I have never been perfect in our entire lives. We've just pretended to be. And we're still alive and kicking!

It's OK to be a mess. It's OK not to have it all together. It's OK to differ from day to day. We imprison ourselves in our "I have it all together" show. Dance, play, sing, move, get dirty in the sand, live each day differently and exactly as you want to. Asking for help is not a weakness. Asking for support is not a weakness. Trusting is not a weakness. Expressing your feelings is not a weakness. Being unapologetic about your desires is not a weakness. Surrendering to the moment is not a weakness. In fact, it's quite the opposite. Only the strong can be truly flexible and vulnerable in an authentic way.

Perfectionism prevents us from being real. The real world isn't perfect. When we admit what is already true about ourselves, we can connect to ourselves and to other people. Leaders of Change are fully human, authentic, and unapologetic about the near misses, the missteps, and the better-luck-next-time realities of life.

Compassion and the Inner Critic

The strongest critic you will face will *not* be any of those around you complaining about how you're never there for them anymore or how you aren't a caring person like you used to be. Yes, you'll hear those voices—plenty of them. But the most powerful voice will be the negative one that resounds loudly inside your own head. This voice believes the lies you have been taught. There's a part of you that tells you you're not good enough, you'll never make it, you're not pretty enough, and you don't deserve any special care. That voice is terrified you'll rock the boat.

You may be hoping that I have some trick for getting rid of the inner critic. Unfortunately, I believe the negative voice will always be with us. Whenever we move beyond our comfort zone, it'll pop up to say, "Go back! You can't do this! Who do you think you are?"

Sometimes it helps to give this voice a name and a character. I created mine in a coaching workshop—her name is Miss Bitch, and she has a stern voice, a tight bun, and frown lines around her mouth. Her Medusa look could turn you into stone. She's the teacher with the ruler in her hand who is there to remind me on a daily basis that I am not good enough.

The voice of the inner critic can say anything it wants. You are not obligated to listen. In fact, you must not believe it. Simply be aware of the voice, and go on with your life. I cannot emphasize this enough. Being aware of your inner critic and not buying into its message is a significant part of the process.

When the voice pipes in, observe it. Notice when it whispers fear and discouragement, when it screams and throws tantrums. What choices does it warn you against? What change does it want to keep you from making? You'll see a pattern. But understand that, in its own misguided way, this part of you is trying to protect you. It's just that it's no longer needed, since you are an adult with intelligence and coping tools, and therefore the dangers it warns about are no longer so dangerous.

Compassion takes the meanness out of the inner critic. It's like the scene from a horror movie when you see the shadow of something huge and scary approaching, only to shine a flashlight on it and realize it's a peewee of a mouse that's strolled up to say hello. That flashlight is compassion.

We have the capacity to make things easy or difficult on ourselves during this journey. The lost treasure map of compassion reveals a vital route to ease and grace. Over time, the voice will lose its power. With greater ease, you'll be able to push its warnings and threats to the side and move forward. Then you won't have to waste time pretending to be perfect. I am real. You are real. We can be beautiful, messy, unapologetic. You have been cut off from the inherent energy of the universe. When the dam is cracked, the water flows to us and through us and beyond us as we become of service to the world.

Ava's Story

Ava had a mop of red curls and big, bright almond-shaped eyes—she seemed innocent and childlike in her demeanor, despite her age. She reported that her mother was constantly criticizing her and that she could no longer tolerate her mom "barking" at her. As soon as Ava walked through the door, her mother's running commentary began before Ava could even say hello. Ava was exhausted and depleted by it and had begun to go out of her way to avoid her mother.

Together Ava and I did some role playing. Ava took on the role of her mother, while I took on the role of Ava. As soon as Ava stepped into her mom's role, she instantly radiated the energy of a wise older woman. She seemed sturdy, like an oak tree that had seen life and withstood the test of time. She looked at me (as I was playing the role of Ava) and said, "I see a mountain of garbage around you. I want nothing more for you than your stepping up and becoming the woman I know you can be. You are already that person. There is nothing to achieve; you just need to let go of the lost little girl you believe yourself to be."

As Ava, I felt every single one of the mother's words reverberate through my body. There was a voice shouting inside my head, and I discovered that the mother's voice was nothing but an echo of the inner critic's voice that I refused to listen to.

We stepped out of our roles. "How unhappy are you?" I asked Ava. She burst into tears. "I've been avoiding that critical inner voice," she admitted. "And I've been projecting it onto my mom." She realized that she'd gotten too comfortable playing a lesser version of herself and that she would have to step up—something she didn't yet know how to do.

External situation: *I can't bear to be around my mother.*

Damsel response: *It's my mom's fault—she's always so critical.*

Superwoman response: *I'll just avoid my mom. To hell with her.*

Leader of Change response:

Self-reflection: How am I critical of myself? What is that critical voice trying to tell me?

Self-love: Can I listen to this critical voice with compassion? Can I develop enough self-awareness to choose not to believe everything it says?

Find the Golden Nugget

Neither the Damsel nor the Superwoman can circumvent the voice of the inner critic. The Damsel cries out to be rescued, and the Superwoman tries to outrun it—both methods that will get them nowhere.

Remember, life is not happening *to* us but *for* us. After lots of self-observation, one thing became clear to me—the inner critic, though often unkind, might just have a gift to share. Within its ugly words, there lies a golden nugget of wisdom. And the Leader of Change extracts the gold and leaves the muck behind.

Say, for example, that your inner critic is constantly berating you for your weight. All cruelty aside, are you happy with your weight? Put aside society's unrealistic expectations on the matter—how do *you* feel in your body? Do you feel good in your body? Is fitness a priority? If not, can it be one?

In this strange, sometimes painful way, the inner voice is helping you to define yourself beyond the world's standards. It is there to propel you to get to know yourself, to strengthen your self-definition.

From the criticism, you can pluck the golden nugget and leave the rest behind. And there is *always* a golden nugget.

Amira's Story

Amira came to me complaining of feeling stuck in life. She suffered from sheer exhaustion, part of her perpetual cycle of burnout. No matter how hard she worked, she was unable to make progress in any area of her life. In fact, she felt as if she were going in circles.

We worked on creating a character to describe what was holding her back. She described an ugly, wrinkly, short, hunchbacked creature wrapped around her legs, preventing her from moving forward. He was sneaky and manipulative, and every time she wanted to push ahead, he got louder and even more manipulative. She named him Gollum, since he was so much like the character from *The Lord of the Rings*. He was determined to keep her in a state of confusion and to remind her that she was not good enough to achieve her goals and that even when she did achieve them, she was unworthy of them.

We explored all the ugliness Gollum was so happy to spew at a moment's notice. Was Amira unworthy of her goals? She retorted that not only was she good enough, but she was "bloody brilliant" and more than worthy of achieving them. But she drove herself to exhaustion, because that was the only time she couldn't hear her inner critic.

Exhaustion was the heavy price she paid for silence. Yet it was in silence that she could listen to herself and access a deeper potential. The nugget of wisdom amid the ugliness was that her self-confidence and self-worth needed a boost.

Amira no longer wanted to live in the exhaustion cycles of her former Superwoman self or be Gollum's confused victim; instead, she would learn to find stillness and balance, to find her own flow and follow it.

External situation: *I can't make progress in my life.*

Damsel response: *I'm just too tired and burned out. I'll never be good enough to achieve anything.*

Superwoman response: *I'll just push through, darn it!*
Leader of Change response:

Self-reflection: I am worthy of my goals, and I can figure out a better plan for moving forward if I put my mind to it.

Self-love: What is the golden nugget within the criticism?

Find Your Voice

To be human is to feel. The depth of human experience occurs within the realm of human emotion.

Once you are back in your body, you will feel the richness of emotions.

Along with those feelings, we must also regain our ability to speak—and I mean this literally as well as figuratively. As children, some of us were told to be quiet, to hush up, to be seen and not heard. Now, I'm not advocating that parents relinquish their responsibility to teach children when it is appropriate for them to talk, but I am advocating that we help children learn to communicate effectively. If we were silenced as children, we must learn to speak up in the literal sense as adults.

And we must reconnect with our ability to speak the truth. To speak *our* truth.

Our truth may have been muffled not only through trauma but by the water we swim in—our upbringing, our education system, society, peer pressure, the media, and cultural beliefs all bear down on us from every direction. This may result in no longer knowing what it is we want to say. When you first come back to your body, something strange may happen: you may find a lock around your heart. Unlocking it requires dealing with your stifled emotions.

Dealing with these emotions allows us to drop our unnecessary baggage. Aren't your shoulders heavy from the psychic load you've been carrying? Aren't your hands sore from holding up the mask? Aren't you faint from holding your breath, fearful someone will find out who you really are?

The truth is that who you are behind the mask is so much more beautiful than the perfect person you're trying to project to the world. When people find out who you really are, those who are genuinely capable of loving you will be delighted you've finally shown up.

So tell others what you are feeling. Describe your dreams and aspirations. Say no when you want or need to, and yes when you want to embrace what is offered to you.

Yasmin's Story

I'll never forget the day Yasmin first came to my office. She was the type of woman who would immediately command attention when she walked into a room. There was something about her that I just couldn't put my finger on. She held herself with such majesty that I couldn't help but feel I was sitting with some form of royalty. Her voice was melodic to the point of being hypnotic. And on top of all that, she was so nice that no one had anything to say about her but praise.

Yasmin was indeed the popular girl everyone knew and loved. And she was tired of being overweight. It was a lifelong issue, and she wanted to know why.

After a few sessions, Yasmin revealed that at a young age, she had decided that she did not want to be like her bossy and dominating older sibling. We soon discovered that she had created a shadow version of herself that was meek, timid, and easily adored. She was afraid that if she ever stood in her true power, she would be like her disagreeable sister. To muffle the inner voice that pleaded with her to step into the greatest version of herself, she ate. To repress the power she knew she had, she ate. To hold back the person she knew she was inside, she ate. She had built a people-pleasing facade at the expense of who she really was and fueled it with food.

The prospect of reconnecting with her body petrified her. At first, Yasmin felt like a turtle hiding in a shell. Revealing her soft, vulnerable, true self was too much of a risk.

As she faced her fears head-on, they began to diminish in power, and the lock around her heart started to let go. Slowly she adopted a more healthful lifestyle, from the food (and the portions) she ate to an appropriate exercise routine. She began getting massage therapy once a month from a trusted practitioner to experience another person's touch and to let her body be seen. Over time, her body changed. But more importantly, how she *felt* about her body changed. For Yasmin, losing the weight meant shedding the facade she'd built over the years and reconnecting to her body for the first time in ages.

External situation: *There is something about my body that I would like to change.*

Damsel response: *I can't do it—I've always been this way and will always be this way.*

Superwoman response: *Sign me up for the newest fad diet and exercise program! I'll do it all, and I'll do it fast!*

Leader of Change response:

Self-reflection: How might my lifestyle be contributing to this issue? How might my mind-set be contributing to this issue? Where can I make healthy, sustainable change?

Self-love: What defense mechanisms did I create for survival reasons that made sense at one time? What can I now let go of? How can I provide what I need to feel happy and safe?

—

REFLECTION EXERCISES

We have a few different avenues through which to reconnect with our bodies. Although you do not have to carry the following exercises out in a specific order, I recommend doing all of them.

Be Present in Your Body

Option #1: Set a timer for five minutes. Inhale and exhale. Listen to your breath.

- What did you discover?

Option #2: Set a timer for five minutes. Inhale and exhale. Listen to your heartbeat.

- What did you discover?

Option #3: Set a timer for five minutes. Inhale and exhale. Concentrate on one part of your body. I recommend starting with your feet or another part of the body that is in contact with the ground. Move your awareness to areas of tension. Give those areas love, and see what happens. You may even find that they relax.

- What did you discover?

Which of these three options did you prefer? Keep practicing—when you feel ready, increase the time you spend on this exercise.

Mind Your Language

Language is an excellent way to work from the outside in. Throughout the day, monitor your vocabulary. At the end of the day, write about the kinds of words you use.

- Do you tend to speak in a more positive way or a more negative way?
- How do you speak about yourself and your body?
- What themes show up in your vocabulary? For example, war terminology, demeaning words, self-effacing humor, or excessive apologies.

Name It and Feel It

Monitor your emotions throughout the day. Make a habit of naming and feeling your emotions. Make this a daily ritual. Feel your emotions, allow them to flow through you. Use your voice. At the end of the day, list the feelings—both positive and negative—you hold inside your body.

To go deeper, pick an emotion for a day and observe it in your body. For example, where do you hold anger? Where do you feel guilt or stress or a sense of being overburdened? Where do you feel joy?

Release Pent-Up Emotions

Dedicate a specific activity to the release of an emotion that is burdening you—for example, anger, frustration, grief, or humiliation. There are many activities that can facilitate that release: painting, dancing, ripping up old newspapers, or vigorous exercise such as boxing. At the beginning of your chosen activity, mentally affirm that you are dedicating the activity to the release of your chosen emotion.

Celebrate Yourself

Write down ten things you love or appreciate about yourself at the end of every day. This could be anything: what you do for those around you, a physical attribute, a characteristic of your personality, or something you did particularly well. Do this for thirty days.

Chapter Five

U = Unblock Your Feminine Potential

Who Is She That Flows Through Us?

So there I was. January 1, 2009. A year had passed since that horrible trauma in London, and I was on the cusp of deciding whether I would try to get pregnant again. The odds stood against me. The past trauma stood against me. My genes stood against me.

The doctors had warned there was no way to know whether a baby had the same fetal akinesia gene until the end of the first trimester. Bonding with a child for fourteen weeks, only to find out she or he wouldn't live, is a pain no mother should have to bear once, let alone twice. The pressure from others, including the insensitive "suck it up and just go for it" attitude I got from some, added to my burden. Did I have the strength to reenter a dream that had the potential to, once again, turn into a living nightmare?

I had peeled away so much. The limiting beliefs, the lack of self-love, the facades, the armor, the relationships that had been oppressive. I had shed and shed and shed. I had stripped away the dead layers and allowed a greater version of myself to come forth.

I reflected on all that I had learned. The shift in my life was undeniable. Life was different because I perceived it differently. The world wasn't out to get me. My relationships had a deeper dimension to them. I was doing what I loved to do and feeling fulfilled through the process.

The questions, the unmet expectations, the not knowing, and the possibility that I'd endure another heartbreak swirled around me and within me. Yet somehow, there was a stillness in me that ran so deep that the incessant chatter had no chance of surviving. There was a calm in the center of the storm. Right in the core of my being, there was a version of me with a strength that my conscious self had never known. There, in my core, was a stillness that I had never fully grasped and a level of clarity that I had never experienced.

She, or rather *I*, had always been there, solid and unwavering. I recognized her immediately because I have always known her, yet somehow she seemed like someone I had just met. Graceful and grounded, both beyond and within my everyday life.

I sat in the comfort of my living room, stretched out on my sofa, engrossed in a book. My phone rang. I planted the book on my belly. I rushed through the call to return to reading. I was at the ending after all, the juicy ending I had waded through a trilogy to get to. I picked up my book, ready to jump back in.

And then there it was, a burst of color. I had a vision of a rainbow—every hue and shade of color meshing into the others, surrounding my tummy. My eyes were wide open. I looked straight at it, too scared to blink for fear I'd lose the beautiful sight. I stared until I could stare no longer.

Then it was gone. In that moment, I absolutely knew. There was life growing inside of me, a baby free of the paralyzing gene.

On September 11, 2009, eight years to the day after my journey began, I gave birth to a healthy baby boy.

Unblock the Flow

Because I had overcome so many barriers and opened up pathways into my soul, my feminine potential had the opportunity to flow freely through me, leading me to glimpse the wisdom that seemed beyond my conscious understanding and yet was grounded in solid reality.

The feminine potential is a power that people, both men and women, have feared. I think we fear her because she is extremely powerful, and any power—masculine or feminine—can be destructive if misunderstood or mismanaged. I confess that I resisted her for many years because I didn't understand her. When we come into contact with feminine potential, we are transformed. And transformation can be terrifying.

But right now, most of us aren't letting her through. In fact, we are expending a great deal of effort to keep her out. Let's admit this to ourselves—you and I have invested massive energy, time, and emotion in keeping ourselves safe from her. Imagine the force it takes to dam up a major river—a herculean feat of engineering. We have built elaborate obstacles within ourselves—carefully, forcefully, and deliberately. The healing and energetic waters that were meant to flow naturally through us and out of us have been blocked and have backed up to form stagnating pools. To keep our feminine potential in her place—contained, cut off, and controlled—we must create and maintain the obstacles in our inner worlds.

Once we realize that our feminine potential is meant for nourishment and renewal, for empowering and nurturing, for inclusive change for everyone, we need to do only one thing: unblock the flow. The feminine potential flows effortlessly through open passages. She does not force her way in. She waits until you unblock those areas of your life that have been closed, clogged, and disconnected. It's as simple as that. As you remove what stands in her way and are open and receptive, the feminine potential will naturally course through your life. No big fanfare. No marching band. No loud proclamation. Simply roll one stone away at a time and let the life-giving waters flow. Almost effortlessly, you will become a Leader of Change. It's who you are.

While it may seem effortless once the energy flows, our fear can keep us from unblocking the passages. Don't allow your fear to slow you down. Unblocking yourself means taking an honest look at what you have not dealt with or are avoiding. We need to tap into the courage to step up and be the best we can be. No one is standing in her way but you—and only you can let her in.

When this natural energy flows through you with your conscious participation, the *entire world* can be transformed. The energy starts to transform *your* world and turn you into a Leader of Change. At its essence, feminine potential is creation, as we bring new life to the world. Birth and rebirth.

In fact, when feminine potential flows through you, not only do you have a blank canvas onto which you can paint the life you desire, but you can also create the canvas, the paintbrush, and the paints. You are able to take the lead and tap into this force in a more conscious and dynamic way than ever before.

Feminine potential will naturally flow through us, like water flows through a clean pipe or like a river flows through a valley.

Our attention is not on doing and achieving, but on being and receiving. We are the *receptacle* of power, not the initiator. We allow her in.

Accessing your feminine potential is a layered journey. It doesn't happen overnight. Nor is the journey linear; instead of completing one stage and then going on to the next, you are likely to find yourself at different stages simultaneously. You will also revisit the same lessons you thought you'd already learned, seeing them with different, more experienced eyes each time.

When we function at our optimum level, masculine and feminine power are equally valued and expressed. As women, we strut with optimal impact when we access both our masculine and our feminine energies. For the rebalance to happen, we need to recognize the power that the feminine brings to the table—the feminine potential in her own right, unmarred by history, living in the memories of our ancestors.

Opening ourselves up to the feminine potential will bring us back into harmony. Everyone benefits when each person, man or woman, expresses his or her inner balance. And our society depends on it. Look around you. There's no hiding from it. The old way, the way of living solely out of our masculine energy, just doesn't work anymore.

Your life will come into balance once you unblock the feminine potential and allow her to flow through you. She is waiting for you to bring balance into being. It can, and must, begin with you.

Symptoms of Imbalance

Let's look more closely at how the imbalance disrupts your personal life in three significant ways.

The Headless-Chicken Frenzy

There is a commonly held belief that women are able to multitask. If you've ever breastfed a baby while answering e-mail or tied your child's shoes while talking to a client on the phone, you know that it is possible, though perhaps not ideal. Doing five things at once in perpetuity can eventually put you in a tailspin, a state of being constantly overwhelmed. It may feel like you're getting everything done in half the time, but you might also be running around like a headless chicken. A headless chicken is not a Leader of Change.

Perhaps you run around all day in a mad rush, gulping your coffee while dressing the kids and rushing them off to school. Once the kids are in the right places, you weave in and out of traffic in a fruitless attempt to speed up your commute, in hopes of not being late . . . again. Once you finally get to work, you're already a hot mess, with your mind flitting to and fro. Distractible and tired, you survive until the end of the day with job intact, praying that you'll get home in time to make dinner, feed the dogs, fold the laundry, and read each child a bedtime story. From before dawn until after dusk, you're in a whirlwind of "I have to be here," "I have to be there," "I have to get this done," "I wish there were two of me so I could get all this stuff done!" At the end of the day, you're exhausted. And well aware that it all starts over the next day.

I'll admit, there is a power in this type of frenzy. You get stuff done. Half-assed? Perhaps. However, you spread yourself so thin between work, home, social responsibilities, and fantasies of things you *want* to do that never come to fruition (a frustration in itself) that your potential and purpose get lost in the activity. You simply don't have the time or energy to bring that purpose to life. You have phenomenal ideas for projects that never see the light of day.

We do so much, so fast, without even being aware or taking a moment to stop and breathe. Even if you get a flash of insight, the moment gets lost in the headlessness. Running around like a headless chicken is a choice. Why do so many of us choose it?

There is a payoff for living in a headless-chicken frenzy: a false sense of self-importance. We put ourselves into the center of the lives of those around us, pushing them to be more dependent and less competent than they really are. In fact, we convince them to live smaller lives than they are capable of. A life of frantic busyness hurts us all.

Our frenzied lives might also help us to avoid a quiet in which we'd have to be ourselves. If we find our sense of worth in the masculine trait of achievement, then what are we worth without it? Accomplishment is rewarding and positive when it's in balance with the feminine. But without the flow of feminine potential, when we take a break, we feel empty and confused. It's much more comfortable to be busy than to be authentic, because it's more familiar.

What would happen if we stopped the madness? We would be faced with honesty and choice. We'd have to take a serious look at what kind of life we've created for ourselves. Perhaps we'd discover that we're not living the lives we dreamed of when we were young and that we're making a much smaller impact on the world than we're capable of.

Gabrielle's Story

Gabrielle arrived aggravated and discouraged. She couldn't bring the project she was envisioning to life. She had all the pieces in place—the idea was brilliant, her business plan was solid, the financial backing was lined up, the networks were established. Yet she couldn't convert the project from its paper form to real life.

To top it off, she frequently experienced severe migraines. All her visits to the doctor proved futile; the MRIs revealed nothing. Sometimes she thought her head was going to explode from the pressure.

Gabrielle was the typical Superwoman with a lot on her plate—she tried to be everywhere all at once, doing things for her family, friends, social organizations, and acquaintances. With the amount she got done, you'd swear there were three of her. During our first session we talked about how many hours she had left in a day to work on her business. Granted, she made progress in the planning stage over a stretch of time. She found herself *thinking* about her business night and day, and that tricked her into believing she was *doing* more than she was. But she just couldn't give it the consistent and focused time it needed to get off the ground.

Once she committed to putting the whirlwind of to-dos and business-related tasks swirling in her mind onto paper, the pressure in her head started to ease. She learned that procrastination did not add up to productivity, and she eventually found herself happier and a lot less snappy at people because she was no longer beating herself up internally. And, with some difficulty, she realized that not every responsibility was a matter of life or death and that the world would in fact keep turning without her. So she let go of some of her obligations and asked for more support from family and friends.

Gabrielle chose to contribute to society with her talent and passion. In the long run, she found that her business was still a means of giving, but those who benefitted from her organic-food services also valued it and paid for the enrichment it brought to their lives.

External situation: *I have a plan but can't seem to get it off the ground.*

Damsel response: *I'm just too busy!*

Superwoman response: *I just have to keep powering through.*

Leader of Change response:

Self-reflection: What seed inside of me am I not growing? What inside of me is not getting the attention it needs to thrive?

Self-love: Can I look at my busyness with compassion and still find a way to simplify my life?

Parasitic Relationships

We have been groomed throughout our lives to sacrifice ourselves for the needs of others. As a result, we unwittingly surround ourselves with people who want to take from us. These parasitic relationships can take many forms: friendships, relationships with family or coworkers, and most certainly, our romantic and intimate relationships. Once you recognize the parasitic dynamic, you are likely to see it in multiple relationships in your life.

One of the side effects of giving too much is that it attracts people who *take* too much. It takes two people to engage in this imbalanced dance—one excessively giving and one excessively taking. As the giver, you get sucked dry. It's not long before you feel resentful of the taker. What seemed like loving and giving on your part soon begins to feel like a defeating, depleting, angry way of life.

It's a significant and momentous act of self-love to set up your boundaries and defend them. Deciding to focus on where you will spend your energy is profound. To begin this process, you must recognize that your needs come first.

But let me warn you—there is an irony to this. The more you come into your feminine potential, the more parasites you are going to attract, like moths to a flame. If you haven't corrected this dynamic within yourself, you could possibly end up worse off than you started! At this point, the ability to say no is of vital importance.

I see this all the time in my work. The women who lack self-love often give an excess of their time, love, energy, and resources. When we have gathered people around us who expect more than we can give, we create a situation that can be very hard to alter. The more you love yourself, however, the easier it becomes. While you can't choose your family of origin, you are free to decide who is actively in your life. To strut, you must make conscious decisions about your relationships.

Aisha's Story

Aisha was the perfect woman on paper. She was well educated, an intellectual who was so well versed in current affairs that she could challenge you on just about any issue. She earned an income far beyond that expected for her age, was well dressed, and carried herself with an air of confidence. She was dating a man, and although she was happy, something just didn't feel right. She couldn't put her finger on it. According to her, their relationship was picture perfect: they traveled, they dined in nice restaurants, and they enjoyed similar hobbies. But instead of buzzing with energy and excitement, more often than not she found herself tired and disinterested.

We delved into the dynamics of her relationship. She expressed how they did everything *he* wanted, she dressed the way *he* preferred, they vacationed in the spots *he* liked, and they hung out with *his* friends. She said yes to anything his heart desired. And when she thought about it, she realized that much of their life was financed by *her*. She rarely used the word "no" in any of her relationships—with her boyfriend, colleagues at work, family, or friends. And she was the first person they came to when they needed money—money she did not necessarily have but would go out of the way to supply.

After this realization, Aisha decided to become more assertive in her romantic relationship and ask for things that *she* wanted. Off he disappeared into the night at the first sight of *her* needs. As difficult as the breakup was, she committed to abandoning her mindless yeses and her eagerness to please. She eventually moved on to a more fulfilling relationship where the give-and-take was much more balanced.

> External situation: *Everything seems perfect. Perfect education, perfect job, perfect boyfriend. So why aren't I happy?*
>
> Damsel response: *I just don't know how to be happy.*

Superwoman response: *My life must not be good enough yet!*

Leader of Change response:

Self-reflection: What truly brings me happiness? Am I relying on someone else for my happiness? Does my behavior reflect that?

Self-love: What can I give myself that will bring me joy?

The Scarcity Mind-Set

Another effect of blocked feminine potential is the belief that there are not enough resources for everyone. It's the mentality that it's a dog-eat-dog world and only the fittest survive.

When you're young, you're told money doesn't grow on trees and taught to avoid spending. The underlying message has always been to grow up, get out, make your own money, and acquire as much as you can, however you can. Hustle and put your nose to the grindstone till the midnight oil burns out, then mindlessly buy stuff to show for it.

We are taught this scarcity mentality at just about the same time we can walk. It's funny that we'll wait to a certain age to have the dreaded sex talk with our kids, but we provide them an early understanding of scarcity. We know money and material things don't buy happiness, yet that's exactly what we advocate. We encourage our kids to build themselves a prefabricated existence, to work for corporations that will spit them out faster than they can sneeze.

This is the outward manifestation of an overly masculine view of the world. Conquer, acquire, and triumph at any cost. This means that someone *must* lose. Is this paradigm sustainable? Must only a small elite dominate the wealth on our planet at the harm of everyone and everything else? Can there be only one winner?

Elisha's Story

Elisha was in her midthirties, with light-brown skin and a mane of thick black hair. Her appearance did not give many clues as to her origins, and she dressed in long skirts and brightly colored scarves that added to her nomadic vibe. Her lighthearted nature and sense of humor instantly set those around her at ease.

But all was not so calm below the surface. Elisha was perturbed about her finances, uncomfortable with having possessions. She gave away the money she inherited, and she couldn't even bring herself to occupy the home she owned.

Soon Elisha revealed to me that her mother, Mariam, had lived through the India-Pakistan Partition, a division of what had been the British Indian Empire—with devastating and bloody results. Mariam lost everything in the process—the only home she'd ever known, the friends she'd had to leave behind, and even some of her family.

She'd created a new life in the United Arab Emirates. But by the time Elisha and her siblings were born, Mariam and her spouse had become extremely successful in business. She acquired money and property and used their possessions to build a metaphorical fortress around them. Obtaining money and belongings was her strategy for coping with the trauma of her past and ensuring that her children never endured the same—when she passed away, it was apparent just how much of it she'd accumulated.

Elisha had internalized her mother's worry, and her response was to assume that she too would lose whatever she owned, just like her mother had. So rather than fight to keep it, she would preemptively give it away. Through our work together, she came to realize she was just as resistant to having a relationship, because she had an overwhelming fear of being cheated on. In other words, she worried that any person in her life would eventually be taken away.

Once Elisha explored the idea that there was no fight to keep anything, she could breathe easier around her possessions. She switched off her fight-or-flight mode and implemented the abundance mindset—there was enough for everyone, no one was out to get her, and she was allowed to keep what came to her. She found great relief in accepting ownership of her possessions. And she found joy in what life had to offer her.

External situation: *I can't seem to own anything.*

Damsel response: *Everything will be taken away, so why bother?*

Superwoman response: *I don't need anything!*

Leader of Change response:

Self-reflection: What does "ownership" mean to me? What part of myself have I disowned?

Self-love: What do I truly need to feel safe, loved, and stable?

Fulfillment Is Already Within You

Far too many times in our lives we participate in situations that devalue, demoralize, and subjugate us. Be it from a demanding boss, a possessive partner, or a controlling parent, we accept treatment that is less than what we deserve. We allow so-called friends to browbeat and manipulate us. We put our children at the center of our worlds, which is not where they belong. We allow ourselves to be abused and deprived for only one reason: a lack of self-love.

When we live without self-love, we are never satisfied. The love of our children is never enough. The adoration of our partner is never enough. Not even our finest accomplishments fill the void, which seems to surprise us. How many times have you hit that ideal weight, only to have that nagging voice in your mind still making you unhappy? You get the raise you worked so hard for, but the joy of that moment quickly slips away. You marry the man of your dreams and wake up on the other side of the honeymoon disappointed and bewildered. You are longing for something no one else can give you—a vibrant self-love that is transforming because it is rooted in your true essence.

Without self-love, we're caught in a never-ending pursuit of the latest hair extensions, newest shoes that we *really* don't need, and hottest personal-development breakthroughs. We'll twist ourselves into pretzels following the newest version of an "ancient" spiritual quest. Are you not weary of this race with no finish line? Have you not jumped on one bandwagon after another enough times to know that the parade always leads back to where you started? Fulfillment is already within you.

It starts by taking care of ourselves. This grounds us, allows us to implement the basics of self-love, and sets us up as a top priority.

If you're not taking care of yourself and not putting yourself first, then you're not setting yourself up to grow. Once you're in your rightful place at the head of the table, you can evaluate what's for dinner and who you are dining with. Is there enough to go around? Are your fellow diners replenishing you or sucking you dry? Whom and what would you like at your table? Let's explore this below.

Self-Care: Physical, Mental, Emotional, and Spiritual

Feminine potential is blocked by one word: "Yes."

People ask you for favors. You say yes. Your partner expects you to sacrifice yourself. You say yes. Your boss gives you more work without giving you a raise. You say yes. You meet your children's legitimate needs by ignoring your own. There's no room in your life for the feminine to flow. That space is already blocked by prior commitments and obligations. When you say yes to the demands of the unchecked and devouring masculine, you say no to your feminine potential.

We've all been there—exhausted, resentful, grumbling. What you do for others is not offered in love, and they sense it. Do you think that no one sees the seething fury beneath the surface of your false smile? To unleash the feminine in your life, you must say no to others and say yes to yourself.

Your feminine potential must flow through your life, not in service of your masculine potential, but in harmony with it. This happens when you consciously commit your energy to love—self-love first and foremost.

The natural objection to self-care is that it is selfish. How dare we, as women, put ourselves first, before those we care for? Today most of our daughters have self-sacrificing martyrs as role models and thus learn that they must give themselves up for the sake of all others. Our sons learn that that is what a woman is supposed to be and do. That women have nothing to contribute beyond familial obligations.

In reality, self-care is a form of self-love, and self-love is a selfless act, because you cannot give to others what you do not have yourself. And embodying self-love models for those around us—especially our children—what healthy self-care looks like.

Loving yourself is an act of courage that requires you to step out of everything you were taught to believe and allow the greatest version of you to shine through. You realize that who you are is greater than what you do. You are finally free to create your life—you love yourself enough to recognize yourself as a creator, and you own what you create. Life isn't happening *to* you; it's happening *for* you. You lead, not cower. You move effortlessly, not trudge heavily through each day.

Loving yourself includes taking good care of yourself. I realize how obvious that sounds—but many of us have trouble managing this very first step. The basics of self-care relate to your physical survival: wholesome food, clean water, plenty of rest, lots of exercise. Self-care on an emotional level entails owning and expressing your emotions. It is vital that you learn how to handle your emotions, that you figure out the best strategies for coping alone and sharing with others. Self-care on a mental level can be accessed by monitoring your thoughts. How do you speak to yourself? Are you curious about life, always looking to learn something new, to read authors with different opinions, to make friends with people unlike yourself? When the feminine potential flows, a variety of people will be drawn to you. Reach out and learn about other worldviews. There is no reason to fear exploring new ideas and approaches.

Last but not least, there is a spiritual aspect to your self-care. Let me define "spiritual." It means honoring your own truth, looking deep inside your soul to discover what resides there that is unique to you, and expressing it in this world. In other words, finding your own path. As a Leader of Change, I discovered that the simple things mattered most. The love, the joy, the laughter with those we love. To be true to what we believe and fulfill the purpose we have on this earth. You can have it all—you just have to figure out what that is for you and then commit yourself to creating it.

Positive Relationships

Admitting to yourself that a relationship is not serving you is a very difficult thing to do.

If a relationship is damaging to you or if it is blocking you, then it's time to reevaluate its presence in your life. Let me ask you a question. If you took all the energy you put into your parasitic relationships and invested it in yourself instead, where would you be? Resentful and exhausted at the end of each day and dreading getting up the next morning? Or fulfilled and ready for a restful night's sleep and excited about tomorrow?

If you're in relationships that are taking more from you than they are giving, it is time to redefine them or get out of them without any excuses. If the people in your life aren't embracing and supporting the growth in your life, then it is time to change the people you're around.

One of the most empowering steps I see my clients take is to develop a positive support system. In my work, I have observed those who come to me with a support system in place and those who happen to be without one. Those surrounded by functional families, healthy social lives, and work environments with colleagues they respect have a tendency to take quantum leaps in their growth, unlike those who are isolated from family, have no interest in listening to others' opinions, and don't cultivate peer relationships at work.

If you're broke and hanging out with broke people, your mind-set isn't going to change, nor are your circumstances. Your ability to be a Leader of Change is significantly reduced if your closest friends are living as Damsels or Superwomen. Few of us can rid ourselves of parasitic relationships until we have the support of a network of people who are truly interested in nurturing our best selves. Women thrive when we support each other, rather than tearing one another down because of the deeply embedded masculine view that there is room for only one at the top. When we structure our support systems so we can be honest with other women, we can all put down the Damsel or Superwoman masks.

Being in a supportive network of women teaches us many things. First, when we make time for positive relationships, we have less time for those who are draining and pressuring us. Second, we learn how to receive help from others. This is key to becoming a Leader of Change. There is a natural flow of give-and-take. Your support system will be there for you and have your back when you start to doubt yourself or find yourself falling back into old patterns.

If your friends are also learning how to let their feminine potential flow through them, your success is much more likely.

The Abundance Mind-Set

I believe that there are enough resources for everyone. To attain the abundance mind-set, you need to give up the fight—the fight for what's yours, the fight for who is right or wrong, the fight to prove that your principles are better than someone else's principles. This struggle is often a projection, a reflection of some internal fear, and it keeps us stuck in the "fight" mode of the fight-or-flight response, which can use up all our energy. Are you worried that if someone else's needs are met, there won't be enough left over for yours?

As Leaders of Change, we place much higher importance on being a conduit for abundance—not just for ourselves but for everyone. Money doesn't have to be simply a means to an end; we can reject the masculine approach to money, which is about a desperate or aggressive form of survival. The making of it, the spending of it—both can be a joyous experience, pleasurable because you are experiencing the ebb and flow of life, albeit in the symbolic form of numbers on your bank statement or invoice. The thing is, the more joy you experience, the more the stream of money seems to flow. You can make and spend from a feminine perspective in which financial abundance is joy, rather than a signifier of worth.

Having a healthy relationship with money requires compassionate detachment, rather than obsessive acquisition or rejection. Sit back and evaluate how money in hand can best improve your life and contribute to society instead of how you can add that extra zero to your income. When you combine your purpose with the energy of abundance, you will be harnessing an inexhaustible resource.

REFLECTION EXERCISES

These questions build one upon another, much like a pyramid. If your foundation is weak, everything on top will be precarious as well.

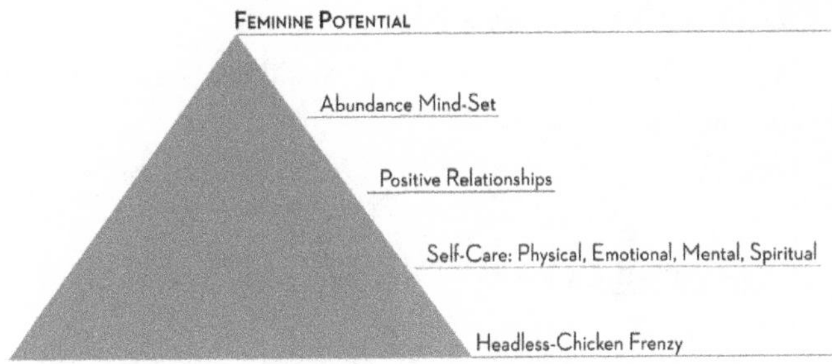

Figure 5.1: The Pyramid of Feminine Potential

Regularly return to these questions to keep yourself on track.

Physical Self-Care

- How does being in a hurried frenzy serve you?
- What does your eating routine look like? Is it well paced or hurried? Are you eating nutritious meals?
- Are you adequately hydrated?

- How many hours of restful sleep do you get every night?
- How much physical activity do you get in a week?
- What are your current commitments? What *really* requires your attention, and what can be delegated?
- What do you say yes to when you'd rather say no?

Emotional Self-Care

- Are you able to effectively communicate what you are feeling?
- Do you express your emotions appropriately, or do you hold yourself back from expressing them?
- On a scale of one to ten, how well do you think you deal with your emotions?

Mental Self-Care

- When was the last time you learned something new?
- What activities do you partake in that encourage your growth?
- Do you surround yourself with people who share your perspectives or people whose perspectives differ from yours?

Spiritual Self-Care

- Are you honoring your own truth?
- How much time do you have for yourself in a day? What does a life of conscious awareness look like?

Positive Relationships

Make a list of your most important relationships. Then answer the following questions for each relationship:

- How much are you putting into this relationship?
- How much are you receiving?
- How does this relationship serve you? How does it serve the other person?
- Is this relationship worth keeping?
- If need be, how can you bring balance to the give-and-take in this relationship?
- Does this person really need you, as opposed to you needing him or her to need you?
- How can you accept more support in your life? What support structures can you put in place?

Abundance Mind-Set

- As a child, what messages did you receive about scarcity or abundance?
- Where in your life do you tend to feel like there's never enough?
- In which situations do you go into fight mode? What would be the alternative?
- When do you feel driven to fight to be right and to prove that the other person is wrong?
- When do you fear your needs will not be met?
- What is your attitude toward money?

Chapter Six

T = Take the Lead

A New Paradigm of Leadership

I sat outside a coffee shop, the warm sun gracing my skin. The hustle and bustle around me was somewhat relaxing. Fashionably attired girls and women dressed in abayas strolled by, their faces pristinely made up and their arms adorned with the latest handbags. Luxury cars passed at speeds slow enough to give pedestrians a chance to admire their beauty.

I tinkered with the spoon that came with my chamomile tea, allowing my thoughts to wander. With gratitude I considered the recent moments in which I'd experienced the power of my feminine potential. Yet I couldn't help but feel that some part of myself was still locked in place.

My mind drifted back to my early trauma, and I wondered what had caused those two teenage girls to mistreat me, a three-year-old, with such cruelty. Why did they choose me? What were they thinking as they watched me cry? Where did they learn to do such horrible acts?

I was suddenly brave enough to explore those questions. Like a bolt of lightning, it came to me: in all likelihood, those two teenagers had been abused themselves.

"Of course!" I muttered under my breath, a knowingness tingling through my body. They acted out the humiliation, the terror, and the helplessness they had suffered at the hands of someone else. Suddenly my heart hurt for them. They had endured what I had endured; they had been tormented as I had been tormented. They had been living out their pain over and over again because they didn't know what to do with it.

In turn, I ended up abusing myself, because I didn't know what to do with the baggage that was passed on to me. I built protective walls around my true self, inadvertently creating my prison. My defense mechanisms stunted my growth and my experience of life. I emotionally did to myself for decades what they had physically done to me for weeks.

With that realization, something lifted from my chest. A boulder of anger that had jammed the entrance to my heart crumbled. I finally understood that I could forgive only from a place of compassion and love, both for those who'd hurt me and for myself. For the first time, I was free of the two innocent girls who had been driven to abuse. For the first time, I faced the darkest part of myself, the part that had been formed because of that abuse and had then gone on to perpetuate it. For the first time, I could love that darkness within them and within myself. And because of that love, that darkness would no longer have power over me, and therefore it would not bleed into my interactions with the people around me who deserve only love.

That moment was like planting a seed of all-encompassing love in what had, with lots of tending, become fertile soil. I'd spent so long uprooting that which did not serve me—the unsustainable drive, the self-defeating despair, the endless swing between frustration and helplessness. Now I could start to truly navigate the world as a Leader of Change, following the guidance of my inner voices, receiving the messages contained within the external reality, and knowing that ultimately they are one and the same.

You Already Are a Leader of Change

For eons women have been fed a story of who we are and who we are supposed to be—a story of worthlessness, violation, and damselhood. We have been told that we are the weaker sex, that we are fit only for supporting roles.

Stripping away the layers of who you think you are can be painful. You may be angry, perhaps very angry, at yourself for not freeing yourself sooner. Facing yourself facade-free, in all your nakedness, can be profoundly upsetting. This newly exposed side of yourself—I'll call her "she"—won't be the pretty picture you've attempted to maintain all these years. She'll be raw, and she might be carrying an incredible store of pent-up anger. And who can blame her? Though all you were trying to do was survive, in essence you colluded with those masculine systems by internalizing them, and in doing so you consented to demean her, judge her, label her, and repress her. She has been held back, reduced into something the world in all its small-mindedness could tolerate. She has been ignored and violated. And she might have something to say about it. By putting down your mask, you might just meet your greatest demon—and she is in fact *you*. You'll have to recognize that you've been both the abuser and the abused, the arsonist and the burned, the murderer and the murdered.

If we come to understand—truly understand, both intellectually and within our very being—that we are Creation and Creation is us, then we must face this part of ourselves that we've worked so hard to disavow. All of us—you, me, the terrorist, the neglected child, the movie star, the refugee—are made of the same material, and we will all return to dust someday. So how you treat others is how you treat yourself, *and how others treat you is also how you treat yourself.* Everything—and I do mean everything—is a reflection and an extension of you.

Now, this is not meant to encourage narcissism—we have enough navel-gazing in this world already. Nor is it to say that everything is your fault or to your credit. That is much too simplistic. I definitely do not want to be a part of blaming the victim, and I'm not denying that there are systems in place that work against you. Every day people rape and abuse and kill and systemically oppress others in so many ways. These are the facts.

Yet it comes down to each of us—in order for us to truly step into our lives as Leaders of Change, we must find the seed of those systems *within our own consciousness*. This is where it starts, for all of us. Because if every single person on this planet decided to face the darkness within himself or herself and work toward love, then these systems would crumble simply because no one was there to uphold them.

To take responsibility for all that exists outside you by looking within can be daunting yet liberating. The falling away of an old story can prompt a profound initial reaction. A paradigm's shifting is like software updating. From the outside, you might look the same as you did before, but you function differently—new and improved. In the process of the reboot, the old and the new might briefly collide as one makes its exit and the other arrives. There is grief in this process. There is resistance in this process. Letting go of everything you believed and knew to be true can be murky ground to maneuver. Before order there is chaos.

How you navigate this new frontier may be similar to the way a child stumbles as she learns how to walk, but the terrain you are in is now totally different. This terrain is free of any story you've ever told the world about yourself. It's free of all your limitations, self-imposed shackles, and the smaller version of you that you have been playing all along. There is an agony here. You miss the old you as you would a beloved. You ache to cling to the known of your former self, but you have come too far to go back. You yearn for the familiar—your victim story, your vocabulary, your belief systems—but none of those ring true anymore. You are orphaned, devoid of anything and everything you have ever known.

And then there is nothingness. A void. Existence as it is. A state so quiet that it's deafening. Let me tell you, it is a very scary place to be at first. You don't know who you are, because you've gone back to the natural version of you that is different from the person the world told you to be. It's scary and unknown. But you learn. Slowly but surely, you learn to exist in this new state.

This is the rebirth process; this is the resurrection. A mourning period is intrinsic to growth. Our former selves deserve appropriate burial rituals; we have to mourn the lives we've lived and find closure. To grow, we shed ourselves bare of what once was.

There is freedom in knowing that no one is coming to save this world we have created, that it is up to us to confront our inner demons so that we can re-create the outer world. The time for this extraordinary task is now. We must stop our world's spiral into self-destruction and make it a better place for those alive today and for our children's children's children—by facing the darkest parts of ourselves with love.

It is time to *know* the truth: you are a Leader of Change.

You could not lead while entrapped in a distorted view of womanhood that gave you only two options: play the victim as the Damsel or carry the facade of the Superwoman. But now, stripped of those pretenses and with the feminine potential flowing through you, you lead.

You have taken the lead by coming into self-awareness, by taking ownership of your life and what you create, and by allowing something deeper—your true power—to flow through you. You took the lead, you set your boundaries, you loved yourself, and you said no to the collective voices outside of you that marred the voice within.

You *are* a Leader of Change.

So now what? How are we supposed to lead from this new place of balance when we have so few role models? Let me share with you what I've learned so far from my own journey and from those of my clients.

Just as change starts within, so does our definition of "leadership." As you reconnect with your body and gather the lost parts of yourself, your self-clarity shifts, and you become progressively more self-aware and confident of yourself as creator of your own life. And as you evolve, so too does your leadership style—you lead others as you lead yourself.

This is not the traditional hierarchical style of leadership, in which subjects are meant to do as their leaders command. Rather, you are a presence that allows all those around you to step into the greatest version of themselves and participate in leadership *with* you. It is like a waltz, in which all the dancers come into sync yet maintain their own rhythm within the collective dance.

This new sense of leadership impacts every interaction in your life, encompassing your children, your partner, your friends, your boss, and most importantly, yourself. By realigning with who we already are, we heal ourselves. And by healing ourselves, we can heal the collective. This is how we will bring about change to the trajectory of the planet. We no longer have to wait for the perfect solution, be it a president, a messiah, or a new belief system, because we ourselves are the key.

You might be saying, "OK, that all makes sense in theory. But does looking at the outer world to see what's going on in your inner world actually work?"

Let's broaden the Damsel versus Superwoman versus Leader of Change responses to go beyond the personal and consider the collective. Here are some examples:

> External situation: *People want to limit the reproductive choices of others.*
>
> Damsel response: *I might as well get used to it—they have control of my body.*
>
> Superwoman response: *How dare they tell me what to do with my body!*
>
> Leader of Change response: *In what ways am I disconnected from my body? In what ways am I giving away my body and my rights? How can I reconnect with my body?*

This idea might seem a little abstract at first, but all it takes is a little bit of practice. Think about the following leadership principles in terms of how they might heal the war within you. If you can apply these concepts—acceptance, authenticity, balance, joy, creative force, and nurturing—to yourself first, then you can apply them to those around you.

Lead with Acceptance

We are part of an infinite web that we cannot see, interrelated in ways we cannot imagine. Once we revert to our original essence, we encounter a paradox: we are all different, yet we are all one. This translates into practical, everyday terms when we take the lead, because in order to do so effectively, we must practice acceptance—acceptance that we all have had different experiences, different upbringings, different exposures to different messaging, different religious rules. The list goes on and on.

Within each of us are wrongness and rightness, darkness and light. Darkness is easier to see when we are looking at others—and so we project outward that which we choose not to see in ourselves. This snowballs into a cycle of hatred, with fingers pointing and no one looking in the mirror. Our children learn whom to hate and how to hate them from us. *Or* they learn that everyone deserves forgiveness, that everyone has the potential for good.

> External situation: *Terrorism is rampant throughout the world.*

Damsel response: *I can't live my life without fear of being blown apart! Let's hide.*

Superwoman response: *To hell with those terrorists! Let's kill them all!*

Leader of Change response: *Whom am I terrorizing? How am I terrorizing myself? How am I contributing to the rise of terrorism?*

The rule of thumb is if it triggers you, it's in you. That's when acceptance of self is called for. Then we can move forward with love to take action with a full and empathetic heart. If each of us accepts the darkness within—which is present no matter how much we deny it and is what makes us human—we can face the darkness of others with clarity and compassion.

Lead with Authenticity

Traditionally, leaders have had characteristics that are valued by society—in today's society, that means charisma, a willingness to listen, extroversion, the ability to take charge, resilience, and so on. The problem with looking to a leader who displays these characteristics is that they can easily be faked. Charisma can be learned, a sweet tongue with empty promises can be mastered, and a willingness to listen can be nothing more than a technique for manipulation, one easily discarded when power is established.

With authenticity at the core of our style of leadership, we no longer have to meet a set list of standards. The impact of authentic leadership is like a stone dropped in a calm pond—the effects spread far and wide in ways that go beyond comprehension. Once we resume power in our own lives, we model healthy leadership for our children and inspire those around us to step up as Leaders of Change themselves. Each person affected in this way further inspires others, and so on. One person is all it takes.

> External situation: *The president is a bully.*
>
> Damsel response: *I'm being bullied, and there's nothing I can do about it.*
>
> Superwoman response: *How dare you bully me!*
>
> Leader of Change response: *What is the bullying dynamic within me? Which part of me is a bully? Which part of me is being bullied?*

It is time that you and I illuminate the world's path in a dramatically differently light. The long wait for change to trickle down from a lone figure sitting at the top, as we desperately hope our voices will be heard over the much louder voices of corporate and political lobbyists, is no longer viable. Leading from a place of authenticity is, now more than ever, absolutely critical. Our planet and our children's futures depend on it.

Lead with Balance

Leadership is traditionally viewed as a sole figure, more often than not a man, who gives direction to those who follow. We use a variety of names for those who lead—trailblazer, groundbreaker, guide, or mentor.

Masculine energy is dangerous when out of balance, but when balanced with feminine energy, it provides critical aspects and capabilities that we need as Leaders of Change. The masculine takes action in a linear, step-by-step fashion toward a specified and measurable goal. The masculine is grounded in the senses and deals well with data and logic. While the masculine potential "does," the feminine potential is the essence of "being." The feminine is collaborative and nurturing in leadership style, trusting her intuition and inner wisdom. She makes decisions collaboratively rather than hierarchically.[16]

Masculine Characteristics	Feminine Characteristics
Do	Be
Linear	Circular
Hierarchical	Collaborative
Goal oriented	Nurturing
Grounded	Intuitive
Rational	Emotional
Self-serving	Connected to the world around her

Having a greater vision without making any concrete plans to carry it out leaves a brilliant idea just as it is: an idea. The feminine charts the course, and the masculine leads the way. Once we let the flow of emotions guide us, it is time for our masculine counterpart to *do* its part. We can *be* joyful and let the masculine translate

16 Elizabeth Gavino, "Balancing Your Dual Energies for Greater Happiness," *Huffington Post,* June 14, 2014, http://www.huffingtonpost.com/elizabeth-gavino/balancing-your-dual-energies-for-greater-happiness_b_5129648.html.

our joy into reality. The feminine and the masculine need to work together to bring about a vision.

> External situation: *Women are undermined in a male-dominated workforce.*
>
> Damsel response: *Oh well, that's just the way the world is.*
>
> Superwoman response: *I'll show them I'm better than them!*
>
> Leader of Change response: *How can I bring my masculine and feminine traits into balance within myself and express them in the workplace?*

Lead with Joy

We have created a world that glorifies being busy. If you're not exhausted, juggling fifteen balls in the air, and constantly complaining about how much you have to do and what little time you have to do it, well, you're just not on the path to success. And if you're relaxed, well rested, and everything is under control, then obviously you're a lady of leisure. Now, what if we were to redefine the benchmarks of success? What if the question was "How much joy do I create around me?"

Once you embrace true strength in all its honesty and vulnerability, you will create room in your life for joy, that exciting rush of vibrancy that flows through your body and lands on your lips, plastering a smile across your face.

External situation: *Women are suffering from burnout faster than men are.*

Damsel response: *I guess exhaustion is just my default state of being.*

Superwoman response: *I'll power through it.*

Leader of Change response: *How am I burning myself out? How can I honor my mental and physical well-being and bring back balance?*

When we lead with joy, it impacts all those around us. Because of your joy, your coworkers, employees, friends, and family will be more joyful too, and their joy will spread in turn. Joy is like a tidal wave—and it begins with one person.

Lead with Creative Force

It takes a man and a woman to create life. But what animates this life? What gives what is essentially a biological and chemical reaction a consciousness, a sense of the world and an individual place in it?

There is a force in the universe that goes by many names, depending on who is speaking. From birth to death, this force brings life to every one of us. At its most basic, it drives us to find food and to seek shelter. At its richest, when it flows freely, it is the very spark of creation.

This creative force washes away our small selves, our private agendas, our superficial motivations. As layer after layer falls away, it gains momentum, eventually reaching our cores, a place where nothing and everything exists at the same time, where the potential of creation is infinite and expansive. It is beyond language—beyond the words "gratitude" or "love" or "compassion." It just *is.*

> External situation: *The economy is failing.*
>
> Damsel response: *How will I make ends meet?*
>
> Superwoman response: *I'll just find another job.*
>
> Leader of Change response: *How am I failing to express my creativity? How can I revamp my business or find a job so that I can express myself creatively?*

The Leader of Change is a vessel for this creative force, which courses out into every action of daily life. A Leader of Change knows that things are created *through* her and not *by* her. She is infinitely powerful, with the power to bring into existence not just her conscious hopes and dreams but also what her conscious mind has yet to fathom. Every molecule in her body seeks to be an expression of this power. She moves and does and leads as though guided by an invisible hand. If feminine potential is the source from which a Leader of Change creates, then the creative force is her form of expression.

Lead with Nurturing

Just as Mother Nature cares for us all, nurturing is an inherent part of each of us. The beauty of nurturing is that it can apply to anything—a child, a vision, a relationship, a friend, or a company. Nurturing fosters collaboration, as everyone is heard, seen, and supported. *No one* gets left behind. Family is no longer limited to bloodlines—you choose who you want to have in your life. Rather than bringing something into existence simply to serve a goal, we both bring it to fruition and envelop it with love. We cherish it and care for it—much like a mother would a child.

> External situation: *The world is full of refugees being displaced and seeking a safe haven.*
>
> Damsel response: *There aren't enough resources here! Look what these refugees are doing to our community!*
>
> Superwoman response: *We're better off without them! Don't let them in!*
>
> Leader of Change response: *Which aspect of myself am I rejecting and shunning? How can I* be *that safe haven that the world so needs?*

Creating a better world in which everyone is safe and cared for comes down to all of us. If you are blessed with food, shelter, and both innate and cultivated intelligence and motivation, then you can re-create this world, starting with the world inside. If you nurture the seed of love within yourself, you will be able to nurture those around you so that they can be the fullest and best versions of themselves instead of who you perceive them to be. It is in the healing of yourself that you heal others. It is in the healing of yourself that you heal the world.

The Road Ahead: A New Paradigm

As you step into your inner world and the global community with your newfound, paradigm-smashing, utterly liberating power, the world might just sense the difference and resist.

You are embarking on a life plan and lifestyle that are uniquely your own. Loving yourself, putting yourself first, and unblocking the feminine potential are completely different ways of being and doing. If you allow balance to come into your life, other people will notice. This isn't a small change. You will be leading your life, setting boundaries and enforcing them. Some people won't be happy about this. Not happy at all.

I say this not to discourage you but to prepare you so that you can stay true to yourself. It is natural for human beings to want things their own way. We all want what we want when we want it. But you and I are taking a completely different path, one that is rooted in authenticity and committed to the betterment of others. We open ourselves up to a profound power by putting ourselves first, knowing that the ultimate outcome will be a transformation for everyone. At least you will offer those around you the opportunity for transformation. Those who choose to stay imbalanced will either leave your life on their own or be contained by your new boundaries. The resistance you'll experience is an indicator that your life is coming back into balance. Don't be surprised by it—expect it.

You and I, as Leaders of Change, are empowered to strut with joy in our hearts, love in our eyes, and clarity of purpose. You understand what it truly means to be a woman. Our greatest gift to ourselves, those around us, and this very planet is to be our best selves. When we achieve this state of being, words like "authenticity" fall to the wayside, because this state is indescribable. When you just *are*, love is not a word, something to be attained or acquired or chased after. It just *is*, as you just *are*. So much power lies in us being this way. And I stress the word "being." In this state, we are the purest form of creation manifested in human form at all times. Being this way allows us to be creators, true Leaders of Change, allowing a new paradigm of consciousness to come through.

Once you reach this state of being, leadership is the ultimate expression of wanting for others what you want for yourself. No more projection of our disowned selves and our need for power over another. Now leadership consists of kindness, compassion, acceptance, and nurturing. Leading this way has a twofold advantage—you allow yourself to heal while holding a space for others to do the same.

There is no more sacred space than this. There is an awe in being alive. A wonder that you were created. An astonishing realization that you are not only harmonious with the song of the universe but a vital part of it. We are Creation, and Creation is us. We are meant to strut, as Leaders of Change, through our own lives and across the global landscape. You can have everything you've ever wanted once you recognize that you *already are* everything you've ever wanted. She's been here all the time.

So what will it be? Will you honor and love your feminine potential enough to be aware of who you let in and out of your life, or will you leave the gates wide open for anyone to come and go as they please? Will you be a Leader of Change or fall back behind the facades? The former choice will allow you to step up, strut, and create a life you love, while the latter will keep you exactly where you are. It's a decision that must be made, one way or the other. What will you choose? Playing it small does no one any service. It is time to take the lead and strut.

REFLECTION EXERCISES

The following questions are meant to help you become a leader. Come back to them often, as your answers are likely to change over time. Don't skim the surface; dive deep for your answers.

- Is there a part of you that needs your forgiveness? Is there someone in your life who has hurt you and who you can forgive?
- Do you tend toward more feminine thinking and behavior patterns or more masculine thinking and behavior patterns? How could you bring about more balance?
- How could you live more authentically? How could you support authenticity in others?
- What in your life brings you joy? How can you bring joy to others?
- Is there anything standing in the way of your creative force? Where would you apply your creative force if it were flowing freely?
- What inside you could use some nurturing? What or whom could you nurture in your life?
- How can you more fully accept yourself—your flaws included? How can you more fully accept others in your life?
- Can you commit to the practice of self-love?

Epilogue

Our Time to Strut

Imagine a world where all women are treated as the magnificent beings that we are. We can walk safely and never come to physical, emotional, or mental harm. Terms of violation are eliminated from the dictionaries and from human consciousness. No mother ever has to lay her child to rest before his time, cross the seas in a rubber boat to a promised land with closed borders, or lose a child to sex trafficking.

Imagine a time when you have all that you need, an abundance that you share with others. Envision yourself with the partner you've dreamed of, someone who loves you and respects you and honors you. Your work is fulfilling, your children are safe, and you wake up every day energized and engaged.

That world is possible. Change won't come from the few who sit on top. Call me a cynic, but I would venture to say that a lot of those folks are hell-bent on *not* allowing that to happen. A world without profit from war, prostitution, drugs, and imperialism is a world where they can't line their pockets at the expense of the majority. They don't have my vote. I have my vote. You have my vote. Every individual woman who chooses to become a Leader of Change by going within to bring change without has my vote.

I matter, you matter, and our children matter. It is our responsibility to bring about the change that the world so desperately needs. One woman stepping into her role as a Leader of Change will allow future generations to follow her example, thus bringing *real* sustainable change to the planet. It takes one empowered woman to allow everyone in her surroundings to step up and strut—and that is a beautiful thing.

Give yourself permission to fall down, get back up, and strut, again and again and again. The journey doesn't end. Keep peeling off those limitations. Every time you come to a new level of being, enjoy it, but don't get too comfortable. Every finish line is the beginning of a new adventure.

And so my journey continues, and so does yours. We already are Leaders of Change, and we continue to become Leaders of Change. We are on a journey of transformation that never ends, at least not in this life. I invite you to join me in changing the world by strutting in our original greatness.

Be the change to lead the change.

Acknowledgments

I am first and foremost deeply grateful to my family and loved ones: My father, who has been empowering me since before I knew what "empowerment" meant, who recognized my greatness in a world that looks down on women, and dedicated his life to nurturing what he saw in me before I knew what it was. I am who I am because of you. My mother, who continually defeated the odds stacked against her. Without you, I wouldn't be standing here today. My husband, who is both my best friend and my life partner. It takes a certain type of man to be married to me, and you're the only one of that kind. You believed in me in my weakest moments, reminding me why I was put on this earth. For that, words cannot express my gratitude. My older brother, who has always helped me brainstorm my way out of a creative ditch. I eagerly await the time when your creative genius will take its place in the world. Sarah, whose invaluable support and guidance, offered over many a karak chai, is immeasurable. My children, who on a daily basis inspire me to be the best human being I can be. My second father figure, Mounir, who loved me unconditionally. Your loss still resonates in my soul.

This book would not have been possible without those who believed in it from the very beginning. Carmen, thank you for being brave enough to venture into my mind and for weaving your magic throughout this book. You have stood by me for years. I love you good. Angela, thank you for the solidarity, dedication, companionship, and laughter, and for believing in this book through the hardest of times. I appreciate you. Chip, thank you for working endlessly to get this book in the right hands. Jessica, thank you for having my back. Anna, thank you for assisting me through the final push with heartfelt grace, courage, and simplicity. Thank you to Erin and her team, without whom this work wouldn't have made it into the world. It has been an absolute privilege to embark on this journey with you.

To the clients I have had the pleasure to work with, to be a witness to your transformations is the honor of a lifetime. You all know who you are. Literally.

About the Author

Photo © 2015 Maha Nasra

Samar Shera earned a bachelor's degree in accounting and finance from the University of Kent in the United Kingdom and studied theology and religious studies at King's College in London. She works as an integrated clinical hypnotherapist and life coach and is certified in energy modalities such as Reiki, Theta Healing, and the Law of Attraction. Brought up in an Islamic Pakistani family living in Dubai, she defies stereotyping and dramatically expands the international conversation about the universal rights, needs, and desires of women and girls. She is married with two young children. For more about the author and her work, visit www.samarshera.com.